YOUR
EPIC LIFE
BLUEPRINT

Quit the Rat Race
and Create a Happier Life!

Rock Thomas

Published by Full Sail Publishing, Chicago, Illinois

ISBN-10: 0-9910823-5-4   ISBN-13: 978-0-9910823-5-3

"In *Your Epic Life Blueprint*, Rock Thomas challenges long-held notions about what it takes to be successful and offers a solid, well-researched action plan that will help you see the world in new ways and change your life."

HAL ELROD,
bestselling author of *The Miracle Morning*

"Rock is the definition of a master. He's travelled the world learning from the best coaches and boiled their wisdom down into his essential rules for success. Read this book as if your life depended on it!"

KRISTOPHER MANCINI,
Get More Coaching Clients, Inc.

"Success begins with the right mindset. Rock shows you how to reframe and rebuild your philosophies so success becomes a habit!"

DAVID OSBORN,
bestselling author of *Wealth Can't Wait*

"This book has it all! The knowledge, the plan, the mindset, and most importantly, the exact things to do to create an epic life! This book is a must for anyone who wants to have massive success."

MARK YEGGE,
author of *Negotiate to Win-Win*

"Rock Thomas does it again! A first-rate book based on an impressive lifetime of research, written in an engaging style, providing just the right balance of intellectual information with practical advice on how to break your bad habits and build an epic life. Rock walks the talk! Now, he'll show you how to live the life you've always imagined."

MICHAEL J. MAHER,
author of 7L: The Seven Levels of Communication

"For those of you who know Rock Thomas, you are already aware of the genuine, abundant life he lives and his ability to help others achieve the same. For those of you who do not know him, invest a few dollars in *Your Epic Life Blueprint*, and allow him to show you what's possible in life and how to grab life big!"

LEN GIANCOLA,
founder of Success Beach

"Inspiring, thought provoking, and life changing! Rock Thomas lays out ten rules to follow to help you reframe your mindset and create the life you want and deserve. Filled with stories of his journey, and helpful action steps, *Your Epic Life Blueprint* engages you every step of the way as you live your journey to an "epic" life."

PAUL ROSSO,
real estate entrepreneur (Bucks County and Beyond)

CONTENTS

A Special Invitation.. 1

Preface... 3

CHAPTER ONE
   Rule One: Schedule time for personal development. 13
CHAPTER TWO
   Rule Two: Build your RRAFT... 33
Chapter Three
   Rule Three: Exploit your gifts, and sharpen your skills.............. 57
CHAPTER FOUR
   Rule Four: Know your hot buttons.. 71
CHAPTER FIVE
   Rule Five: Focus your energy.. 99
CHAPTER SIX
   Rule Six: Nurture your beliefs... 115
CHAPTER SEVEN
   Rule Seven: Increase your net worth.. 131
CHAPTER EIGHT
   Rule Eight: Success is a ritual. It's not owned; it's leased.
   You pay the rent every day with your efforts. 147
CHAPTER NINE
   Rule Nine: Become a master of meaning.................................... 165
CHAPTER TEN
   Rule Ten: Make it happen, no matter what................................. 179

About the Author.. 192
Also by Rock Thomas.. 193

A SPECIAL INVITATION

When I wrote *Your Epic Life Blueprint*, I wanted to do more than just write another book; I'm out to change lives!

The *Epic Life Blueprint* online community is a social learning platform that takes what you'll discover in this book to another level, allowing people like you to connect with an inspired community of like-minded, goal-oriented, fun-loving people who have also committed to building their epic life blueprints! It's filled with motivation, inspiration, love, knowledge, and support to help you reach the goal you've committed to.

I'll drop in to post additional resources, host live chats, answer your questions, and cheer you on.

JOIN THE EPIC LIFE BLUEPRINT COMMUNITY
www.facebook.com/groups/YourEpicLifeBlueprintCommunity
Currently accepting members. Click "Join Group" on the
Facebook page

Check out my website for additional tools, new content, videos, and webinars designed to help you live the life you've always dreamed of. Or connect with my mastermind groups M1 and Gobundance. One click and one choice could literally change your life.

Free Bonuses

10 Steps to 10x Your Life eBook
and the *Rise with Rock* podcast online library
(21 shows and growing)

Get them NOW at rockthomas.com

You can also find me on Twitter, Facebook, and Instagram. Please send a message, leave a comment, or ask questions. I do my best to respond to everyone who contacts me, so let's connect!

Invite a Friend

Research shows you're more likely to achieve a goal if you have a friend join you on your endeavor. Invite your tribe to join your new adventure!

Kudos for taking the first steps toward a braver, bolder, more successful, and happier life. I can't wait to hear about your experiences!

With love and gratitude,

Rock

PREFACE

I wrote *Your Epic Life Blueprint* after several people asked me how I'd become so successful. Their questions, and my desire to help others, prompted me to stop and think about it, write things down, and share the secrets of my success.

Before you Begin; you Should Know This is not Your Typical Book.

Your Epic Life Blueprint is not so much a self-help or personal-growth book as it is a personal change *tool*. Each life blueprint you create (and you can create as many as you need) will be as unique as you are. Through exercises and actions, you'll be forced to rethink many areas of your life that have been running on autopilot. This disruption of your comfort zone will either totally freak you out or, if you go with it, totally change your life.

So, why did I set out to make this book so different from others? I could have written just another standard motivational book, so why write one I knew would only appeal to people ready to make massive changes in their lives?

After writing my first book *The Power of Your Identity*, I spent time as a snowbird in Florida. I played a great deal of golf and rubbed elbows with many successful people. Every time I came back to Canada, I saw people working more than full-time hours, for themselves or others, yet struggling to find success.

Financially free by the age of forty, I wondered why some people achieve success while others never find it. I thought about the questions people asked about my accomplishments and how the right answers could help them. I also thought about everything already out there and realized that the key isn't so much motivation as it is *action*.

How This Book will Propel you from Motivated to Life-Changing Action

- You'll uncover hidden beliefs holding you back and powerful questions that will supercharge everything you do.
- Procrastination and roadblocks will vanish once you get the "why" about what matters most in your life.
- Willpower alone seldom works. I'll teach you how to conquer mental and physical fatigue and build momentum toward your goals that will astonish you.
- Stunningly simple tactics will guarantee you finish projects that matter most to you, resulting in 10x your productivity.
- Crystal clear logic you'll come up with yourself will help you stick to it, even when the going gets tough.
- Discover smart ways to deal with toxic relationships so you can form new and better support systems to rocket you forward.
- And…so much more.

> *Unlike with other personal development books, "Your Epic Life Blueprint" inspired me to do more than read and say, "That's good. I'll do that later," then put the book down and never do anything. I love all the calls to action. They called me out, made me squirm, and inspired me to finally do something to create changes in my life!*
>
> **– PAMELA TURNIER HORN**

After looking at what worked for me and talking with some of the most successful people in the world, I came up with ten "musts" for success—ten principles—that when acted upon consistently resulted in measurable increases in performance and higher levels of success.

When I'm off track with these principles, I slow down and feel sad or discouraged. Success, effectiveness, and happiness slip away.

Lightbulb moment! **I'd learned the most important lesson of all...*how* to create lasting change.**

That's why I am so excited to share the success principles that work for me, other consistently successful and happy people, and my best mentors.

I'll also share what doesn't work. Even successful people struggle. The lessons we've learned through our failures are valuable too.

In ten short chapters, you'll learn the rules, why they work, and the compelling science behind them. Building your epic life really is as simple as hacking yourself to discover what works best for you. **Today, too many people operate using old software. This book is your upgrade. Your personal call to action.**

> *Rule #4 changed my life. Despite being a person who loves adventure, I realized I'm more comfortable in my "comfort zone". The risk of changing scared me. Once I got comfortable at not being comfortable, drastic changes happened. I went bungee jumping, backpacked Costa Rica, and kayaked with crocodiles! Now that I'm part of the Epic Life Blueprint Community, this is just the beginning.*
>
> *– CODY VOGHT*

Success isn't elusive or exclusive. It's not a riddle or puzzle with a lucky few people holding the clues. Success is more like building a house. When you follow a well-crafted blueprint, the results are consistent and easily duplicated. *Your Epic Life Blueprint* **will give you a personalized success plan to wake up your fearless inner rock star, genius, giant, best version of yourself.**

> *Living my life by the ten rules and focusing on my blue-print, I've more than doubled my passive income. I found out who I was in my core and overcame many limiting beliefs that held me back from being the person I really wanted to be.*
>
> **– DIEGO CORTEZ**

Unlike some "self-help" books, *Epic Life* gives you more than advice. You'll get a clear success blueprint template to follow, ten easy habits to incorporate into your routine, and simple instructions on how to build a new and epic life.

As you create your personal blueprint, **you'll see rapid results, whether you focus on financial freedom, better relationships, increasing your energy level, becoming healthier, or tackle several areas at the same time.**

I've struggled with these things too. Yet, today, I'm blessed with abundance in all parts of my life.

In the early 90s, I wasn't making ends meet. My father was ill, and I'd been let go from my job. I ran through my money helping my dad, and my landlord evicted me from my apartment. Though my life was in turmoil in almost every area, I gathered up the shattered pieces and cemented them together using the ten principles I'll outline for you.

Before the bottom fell out of my life, I dreamed of becoming a successful real-estate sales professional and the owner of my own franchise. With nowhere to go but up, I decided to get into real estate as a residential agent and learn the ropes from the ground up.

Within five years, I bought the largest real-estate company in the province of Quebec, ran it for ten years (with increasing sales and revenue every year), sold it, and retired.

I gained the freedom to do what I love to do—help others. I wrote a book, produced educational audio programs, and traveled around the world studying with others and empowering people to find new levels of success.

How did I do it? How did I do it so quickly? How did I turn my life around? What did I learn while studying with many of the world's leading mentors, yogis on mountaintops, and wildly successful business people? What's the real secret to building "whole-life wealth" (a life where you're happy and successful in all areas, free to do whatever you dream of doing)?

I'll share the distilled wisdom I learned from countless world-class experts, handpicked from hundreds of top authorities on happiness, health, money-management, balance, success, and productivity. Many of these experts charge thousands of dollars for their time. But, in this book, you'll get their best strategies and tools for living at a fraction of the price.

> *Rock, you have mentored me into who I am today. Your absolute certainty about taking on any challenge has rubbed off on me in the best way possible! I feel strong, unstoppable, and at peace with myself. I've developed rituals that keep me in constant progress mentality, utilizing all my passion and energy toward massive action. I hope it makes you proud to know that this once hesitant kid is leaping over any challenge that comes his way and helping others do the same.*
>
> *– ALESSIO DEL PAPA*

Like everyone, I have challenges too. Success doesn't eliminate obstacles or problems, but the quality of your problems changes. Now, when I hit a landmine or pothole, I make rapid corrections using the skills and behaviors I learned to get back on track.

Life will throw you curves, whether they come from family, friends, the economy, or your job. You need to have something to fall back on you know is going to work, especially when you find yourself struggling. You need a solid foundation and a lifeboat when you start to feel like you're drifting aimlessly. You need a set of instructions and a simple plan. You need to know if you follow your plan, success will come. **These rules act like "set points" and help you stay on track no matter what. This book will give you a clear and actionable plan and wake up your inner change agent.**

> *RRAFTing my big goals (rule #2) keeps me purposeful. Rock's accessibility through the Epic Life Blueprint Community and M1 is amazing. Missing the opportunity to talk with him and hundreds of other successful people would be shameless. Thank you, Rock, for sharing your story and the lessons you learned, so the rest of us can take a shortcut. You are an absolute badass!*
> **– EMANUELE PANI**

Before we get started, I need to make a couple of agreements with you.

First, commit to following through with the ten rules outlined in this book. We're all busy, so it's easy to start something and be knocked off-path, like joining a gym and never going.
One of the principles of success is completion. Too many people stop three feet from winning gold or from completing a goal.
But winners always find a way to finish. Losers find excuses. Harsh, but true. Winning doesn't mean always coming in first. Simply finishing a twenty-six-mile marathon is a huge success for anyone.
If you want to find success as a result of completing the plan in this book, make a commitment to yourself before you continue reading. Commit to applying what you'll learn. In some cases, you may need to complete an exercise. This might mean trying something different.

Whatever it is, however you feel about it, agree to complete your blueprint.

Second, pick an accountability partner, and join my mastermind group (M1) where you'll be held accountable and helped to build your epic life. The more people who go through this process with you—to enrich your experience and hold your feet to the fire when you get off track—the better. Of course, you'll do the same for them. Partnering with others will enhance your experience and dramatically increase your odds of completing your blueprint.

Talk with your partner about each chapter and clarify your intentions and decisions. When you make your intentions known, remarkable things happen. Answers to your questions become available, and resources appear. New energy propels you toward your goals because you shared them.

> *Since sharing my dreams with Rock and my accountability partner, I'm completely excited about the upward trajectory in my life. Rock helped me identify areas I didn't even know I needed to work on! No matter where you are in life—at the top or at the bottom—do yourself a favor and take action.*
>
> *– BEN LEE*

Don't skip this important step. Find an accountability partner, and look into M1 right now to connect with a tribe marching to millions of dollars of net worth without sacrificing their health or their relationships.

If your net worth is more than one million dollars already, and you're looking for a mastermind group, check out the high-net-worth group Gobundance.

Not ready for that yet? Then join the Epic Life Blueprint Community on Facebook where you can lurk and learn or participate and grow. Once you've worked your blueprint, do yourself a favor, and share your successes with the group. There's nothing like the joy you'll feel helping others find ways out of places you've left in the dust.

Third, agree to have fun as we go through this process together. Like we're hanging out having a conversation, I'll be open and honest while sharing the ten principles that created positive results for me and thousands of other successful people.

Action Step

- **Find a journal to use as a companion workbook for *Epic Life*, or write directly in the book. Write the following and their answers:**

My accountability partner is:

_____

Groups I joined are:

_____

_____

_____

Are you ready to rock?

Find a comfortable place to relax, grab a pencil and your journal if you're using one, and prepare to draft your epic life blueprint and build your road to success!

CHAPTER ONE

Rule One: Schedule time for personal
development.

*"We cannot solve our problems with the same
level of thinking that created them."*
Albert Einstein

Your most valuable asset is your mind—the programming inside
your brain and the thoughts you think. Thoughts manufacture
emotions, and emotions lead to your actions.

Unfortunately, humans are conditioned by an irresistible temptation to hold onto negativity. As with a garden, the harvest you reap is
directly proportional to the seeds you sow and the care you provide.
If you don't remove weeds from your garden, they'll overtake your
crops, and you'll have a poor harvest. If you don't weed out negative
thoughts in your mind, you'll produce negative results in your life.
What you have habitually harvested as emotional past patterns, you'll
reproduce in your future.

I didn't always know this or believe it, but I started becoming
aware of the principle at a young age (whether I wanted to or not,
thanks to my dad). When I was growing up, we didn't have a television, so I spent a lot of time reading. Though I didn't see it then,
books taught me many ideas, a love for learning, and gave me a huge
advantage over many other people.

Now, I read more than I watch television or surf the internet. I've realized personal development is an ongoing pursuit. You can't do it occasionally, when the mood strikes. You don't eat once a year. You don't shower once a year either (hopefully), and you don't cut your grass once a year. Your grass grows; you cut it. Your hair grows; you cut it.

Just like weeds, grass, and hair, negative thoughts will grow whether you like them or not. It's up to you to cut them out of your life. You must weed your mental garden regularly.

Many people fall into the trap of leaving their mindset to chance, believing their thoughts are random—they are what they are and can't be controlled. They think, "I can't change my thoughts. I am who I am, and I think what I think, and what difference does any of it make? None."

If you find yourself held back by thoughts like these, you'll benefit from weeding them out starting today, right now. If you don't consciously make a change, you're accepting that your future will be just like today as you repeat old habits and go nowhere. You can accept the obstacles life throws at you and resist change or you can develop habits and skills leading to the easy success you desire. You can develop methods to program yourself to change by focusing on your goals in new ways.

Choose goals enabling you to grow and evolve into the successful person you know you can be.

The choice is yours. So, don't wait. Do it now. Educate and inspire yourself.

Action Step

- **Take a moment to write in your journal ideas that have resonated with you so far or record them below. Continue to do so as you find other inspiring ideas. Highlight them, and read them often.**

In Napoleon Hill's classic book *Think and Grow Rich,* he discusses his theory about thoughts being things and shares his conviction that we can manage our thoughts.

Throughout our lives, we're instructed and advised by our teachers, parents, uncles, aunts, and neighbors. We're fed messages by traditional media. Over time, we think things without knowing why we think them. We forget to ask why. We become numb to the negative thoughts dogging us. We unconsciously endorse our thoughts and accept them, giving them permission to run our lives, and we don't add new thoughts that will work better for us.

We have an average of 60,000 thoughts a day. Yet, 95% of them are the same, day after day! If you aren't where you want to be, then guess what? It's time for new programming. Your situation isn't going to change unless you change your inputs, and give your mind new information. Therefore, scheduling personal development is an absolute must for long-term success.

Nothing changes until you change, and when you change, everything changes.

Science says your brain is not responsible for making you happy. Your mind has one job—survival. When you're in the woods, and you hear the crack of a branch, your mind doesn't assume someone's coming to give you a bag of money. Your brain triggers an alarm in case a bear is coming to kill you. It suggests danger first. Always.

The reptilian part of your brain (or the "monkey mind" as some people call it) has not changed much in thousands of years. It still employs the same chemicals and operating systems activated by humans' fight or flight instincts. Adrenaline and cascades of hormonal secretions occur for everything from traffic jams to contracts that might not be renewed. Because of the brain's inability to distinguish between real or perceived dangers, we're bombarded with fear and worries about death over non-life-threatening events.

Studies show meditation, breathing exercises, and awareness about your patterns of reaction will dramatically affect your well-being for the better; however, in this chapter, I want to underscore your need to adapt your software (the programing of your mind) to bring you into the 21st century. You're not stuck with what the brain wants to do. You can change its patterns and, subsequently, your thoughts and behavior. But, first, you must make the all-important promise to yourself to follow through.

One key to making the commitment to schedule your personal growth efforts is to first expand your view of what personal development is. Some folks resist the idea of learning new skills because learning new things reminds them of school. We spend a large part of our young lives going to school and, as an adult, perhaps you feel as though you've had enough.

Or maybe you're sick of self-help books that haven't helped at all.

Start with areas of interest and topics that get you excited right from the beginning. When you love what you're doing, it doesn't feel like work, right? So, dive into these new and exciting areas first. Incorporate a blend of topics you're drawn to along with new or more challenging topics you know will require more attention and skill building.

It's helpful to incorporate different styles of learning too. Read books and articles. Listen to audio programs and podcasts. Watch videos on YouTube and TED Talks. Dive into roll-up-your-sleeves, hands-on experiences.

We learn at different rates and in different ways and will naturally favor one form of learning (auditory, visual, or kinesthetic) over others. If you're an auditory learner, you'll absorb information best when you listen to programs. You may wish to consider purchasing the audiobook version of *Epic Life*.

Every time we stretch our boundaries, even a little, we grow bigger, better, faster, stronger, and capable of absorbing and processing more new information.

You were designed to learn, and you'll be happier in a state of curiosity, absorbing new knowledge. This will keep you entertained and working faster.

Now, think about highly successful people like athletes and entertainers. A common denominator with them is the input they received from coaches, mentors, or others experienced in their field. Working with someone farther down the track than you are can shave weeks, months, or even years off your learning curve.

The Power of Awareness Through Feedback

Feedback is not good or bad, right or wrong; it's just information. Accepting this premise is the first step to being an outstanding student.

A coach, teacher, or accountability partner might begin by holding up a mirror (not always a pretty picture). What you see might hurt at first, but the truth will set you free. It will increase your awareness and allow you to transform old habits that are not serving you into new ones that will.

A coach will hold you accountable. There's something about not wanting to let another person down that motivates us to act even when we might not do it for ourselves. A good teacher will help you make decisions, set goals, and find strategies to overcome obstacles.

An accountability partner or coach will encourage you to celebrate your victories. In the ongoing process of personal development, this step is often overlooked or underplayed. Though humility or social norms might prevent us from tooting our own horns, we're creatures who crave recognition. Yet, we rarely feel validated by our peers or loved ones. Coaches never skip this step.

I enjoy celebrating victories so much, I created a mastermind group to share joy with everyone I know. Members live by certain axioms. One of my favorites is we should not apologize for being awesome. This attitude fosters self-love and confidence. It's not about ego but a celebration of our efforts, worth, and accomplishments.

We'll talk more about that later, but if you'd like to hang out with people like this, go to Gobundance, and read about one of the tribes that will help you embrace the power of celebrating your achievements.

Grab your journal again, and begin a list of achievements you could celebrate right now or write them below. We've all accomplished something. Learn to recognize your wins.

_____

_____

_____

_____

_____

_____

_____

_____

_____

_____

_____

_____

_____

_____

_____

_____

_____

_____

_____

_____

_____

Part of the beauty of setting goals and moving forward is pausing along the way to enjoy the moments and the changing view as you climb higher and higher. It's motivational to look at where you've been, see what you've accomplished, and treat yourself to simple rewards you've earned along the way.

Occasionally, we need somebody else to believe in us. When you're feeling down and discouraged, they'll give you the boost you need to see the part of you that you can't see, to remind you of your potential, and give you hope.

Support and encouragement are crucial to your success and personal growth. You can be there for others too. Be available to help people in areas where you're strong or have experience, and everyone gets stronger and more confident.

A big part of becoming successful is confidence. When you're sure of yourself, people notice. Successful people are good at influencing themselves and others.

How about you? Are you motivated to do what needs to be done when it needs to be done? Your success depends on your willingness to push forward when you're not in the mood, when you're tired, and *Game of Thrones* is on.

You must put yourself first. This sounds simple, but doing this is hard for some people. Once you develop this habit, and see the improved results in all areas of your life, it gets easier.

I've trained my brain to do what needs to be done when it needs to be done. I programmed it for success by absorbing, trying, and learning the most effective lessons from successful people.

Reading this book is a fantastic indication that you're willing to make some changes to achieve epic success and wellbeing.

I coach people all over the world, and many say they're going to do "it" when life gets easier, and opportunities come to them. But life doesn't work that way for most of us.

People tell me they have lists of things they'll get to once "things get better" or easier. Yet, one year roles into the next, and nothing changes.

Everyone has reasons why things aren't going well for them. Lists they produce no matter what happens. They never seem to catch a break.

Life holds unique challenges for everyone. But opportunity doesn't return to houses when nobody answers the door. That's the easiest first step to make. Open the door. Stop making excuses.

The better you handle the easy stuff (like being ready to change), the less challenging hard things will be. So, start there. Start by showing up.

Life moves forward and changes, whether you like it or not. If you relax and understand your only role in life is to grow—your soul, your physical body, your endurance, your resilience, your heart, or any thing else you desire—you'll be eager to begin this exciting journey of self-development.

So far, the actions you've committed to doing have been easy, fun, and in your control. But what if things go off the rails? You can sink into despair and old patterns, or you can keep moving. One minute at a time if you must. First, get back on the train. Easy.

I went through one of those tough times after great successes in the 90s real-estate market. Turbulence hit in 2000 when I had a "Triple EEE" (an extreme emotional event).

There'd been warnings, like a popup on your computer suggesting you download new software, but you don't have time, so you ignore it. Later (soon, usually), you find out you couldn't function without the update. Always happens.

What happened to me was more than a popup. I struggled with my marriage and divorced. My health wasn't where I wanted it to be, and I was off track in many areas of my life. My garden was full of weeds. After making a ton of money in real estate, I thought I was infallible and that everything I touched would turn to gold. I got greedy and lost close to a million dollars in the stock market. Though I'd believed I was on top of the world, I wasn't. I needed to make some changes. Fast. I decided to take a golf trip to Mexico in search of answers and to de-stress.

I always buy a new book when I travel. This time, I picked up a Tony Robbins book and read it on the plane. Right away, it excited me.

When I arrived in Mexico, instead of golfing in the morning and sitting by the pool with a tropical drink (or two or three) in the afternoon, I read. I devoured Tony's book and got goose bumps, excited about my life's potential again. I realized I hadn't updated my software for a long time. And I needed more. By doing this one small thing differently—scheduling time to read self-development books—I'd achieve better results and be happier immediately, the way I'd felt when I read Tony's book.

Too many people wait to be happy. They put conditions on it. Have you noticed when most of us achieve our "happiness event", we move the goal post and need to hustle to achieve the elusive state of happiness that always seems just out of reach?

Reading Tony's book on my vacation was a breakthrough for me because I realized I could take charge of my life by taking charge of my thoughts. I acted immediately.

Over the next eighteen months, I attended nineteen events with Tony Robbins and others, capping it off by hiring Tony as my personal coach.

When I made time for and scheduled personal development activities, my health and energy levels sharply increased. An incredible dynamic unfolded, creating a desire to learn and grow even more.

We schedule oil changes for our cars. We schedule workouts at the gym. Think of personal development as scheduling a workout for your mind. I've studied with the most successful and happy people on the planet, and they're all avid self-discovering students.

Personal development works for everybody because our thoughts, feelings, and beliefs lead to our actions, and our actions lead to our results.

Think about this for a minute. Understand the importance of personal development and what it can do for you. How easy it is.

Your ability to embrace this concept will shape the outcome of your epic life blueprint.

If your thoughts, your feelings, and your beliefs lead to your actions, but your actions are not what you want them to be, then your results will not be what you want them to be either.

Focus. First, on your thoughts then on your actions.

Many people focus more on the obstacles between them and their desired results, ignoring their thoughts and actions.

"I don't have enough money."

"I don't have the right relationship."

"My life sucks."

Negative thoughts, focused on bad results, produces bitter people. They fight back with blame (usually aimed at outside forces) as an excuse for their lackluster results and performance.

Stop Negative Thoughts.

Imagine a tree representing the results of everything you do (or don't do) in your life. The roots under the soil—unseen, out of sight, and often out of mind—support and feed your tree, helping it bear fruit. What if your tree doesn't produce fruit? What do you do? Chop down the tree? Ignore it, and hope for the best? Would it be better to nourish your tree, and feed the root system a diet rich in nutrients, fertilizer, and plenty of water? Wouldn't you make sure your tree is in a good location, with the right amount of sun, and check it on a regular basis before giving up? If you wanted it to live, you would.

But we've all seen people "killing their trees". They make New Year's resolutions and break them. They try to increase their income by starting a new business then fail because they went off half-cocked with no plan. They change their partners but always have the same problems in new relationships. Why? Because their thoughts, feelings, and beliefs (their roots) keep producing the same fruits—their results. Their pattern of actions creates the same results, year after year.

Nothing will change in your life until you realize that all change must start at your roots. If you keep doing the same things you've always done, you'll continue to get the same results.

Only change produces new results.

I'm talking about permanent change. Change that will give you long-term, lasting success in any area of your life.

It takes consistent weighing of your thoughts to be successful in life. To do this, you must pay attention to the area you have the greatest control over—what goes into your root system—the inputs you choose, the books you read, the audio programs you listen to, the videos you watch, the classes you attend, and the people you associate with.

Just as you don't leave your garden to fend for itself under some haphazard watering system, you must commit to regular maintenance and improvement of your root system—your mind. You must take charge, schedule, and experience the joy of personal development.

I've recently taken up meditation and travelled to India to spend time with people in a culture that has been studying meditation for thousands of years. Why? Because working with the best saves time spent on trial and error, and I don't have time to waste when it comes to making my life better.

When I wanted to improve my golf game, I hired the same guy who taught Tiger Woods.

When I wanted to become a better speaker and coach, I hired Tony Robbins and T. Harv Eker.

Now, I seek happiness, fulfillment, and for ways to crack the code so I can access my full potential and help others do the same.

If you've already found your path, you wouldn't be reading this book. So, let's agree to nourish our minds consistently from now on. Deal?

Action Steps

- **Grab a different audiobook or program, and load it into your mobile device.**

Go ahead. Do it now. Put this book down, and go find another interesting and motivational audiobook or program.

New results come from breaking current patterns and establishing new ones. Studies show 90% of people don't finish reading books they purchase. Odds are, you have some laying around. Pull your choice out, put it in your car, by your nightstand, or in the bag you take to the office every day. Go shopping at your favorite online store and download something if you don't find anything that gets you excited.

If you learn best by reading, read something old and treasured, something you enjoyed before. Something that inspired or motivated you. Re-reading a good book can be more powerful than reading a new one. Read with a highlighter and mark passages that resonate with you the most. Today's electronic reading devices allow you to highlight and note text too. When you re-read a book, read the highlighted parts.

- **Grab your calendar and start scheduling your personal development, though you may be thinking, *"Rock, I'm already so busy. How am I going to do this?"***

First, you need to revisit your commitment to getting better results, and remember the promise you made earlier to do the things I'm inviting you to do. Then, think about your net time. And we're not talking about that much time either. You can find time.

No Extra Time

You can accomplish more, with the same amount of time, by taking advantage of your downtime.

You may be saying, "I have no downtime!"

Look again.

We spend roughly three years of our lives waiting in line.

The next time you're waiting in line at the bank, or you're on a plane, or in an elevator, listen to an audiobook or read a book.

When I play golf alone, I walk down the fairway reading a book. That might seem extreme, but it illustrates that you can find time to infuse your mind with inspiration if you're committed.

If you can't find the time, examine your excuses.

Get into the habit of carrying a book with you. Fit in reading when you're in the bathroom or before going to sleep at night. Find time for at least a half hour for your personal growth every day. Look for ways to maximize downtime to program your mind for success. Or you could waste precious time playing hours of video games, gossiping, and sighing about how life is boring and hard, and about the things you'd do if you had time! When you look at it this way, choosing you doesn't seem to be much of a choice at all.

If you're still having a hard time with the idea of planned personal development, ask yourself if you're curious. Are you in a state of mo mentum or stagnation when it comes to growing your mind and spirit? Then, look for free time again.

Successful people are committed to making things happen and are willing to be creative to get outstanding results. If you do what everyone else is doing, you'll be average. That's not what you want or you wouldn't be reading *Epic Life*.

If you're still resisting or lamenting your lack of time, it might not be the idea of personal development that troubles you, but the execution. Remind yourself that you're in charge. You're the boss in your life. We all have the same amount of time to spend each day. Once you commit to spending yours more wisely, everything will fall into place. So, let's find the time.

Most people spend an average of four-and-a-half hours in front of the television every day! This may not be you, but I bet you could swipe some time from this activity in exchange for some personal development.

- **Learn while driving at least 50% of the time.**

Maybe the easiest place to find downtime is time spent in your car;

the average is an hour a day. Create a rule—50% of the time you're in your car you listen to a personal development audiobook or program.

If you don't like this idea, remember your net worth will not grow more than you do. If you need proof, look at the most successful people in the world. They don't listen to the radio in their cars. Ever.

Once, a young man and his mom came up to me at one of my seminars. "Hey, you da man!" the teenager said.

Flattered, I replied, "Thank you!"

"No! You're the man in the car. I have to listen to you all the time because you're all my mom plays!"

We laughed, but I was happy to know his mom had acted upon my suggestion. I was thrilled she'd shared the practice with her son and to hear the results they were enjoying together.

Commit to listening to inspirational audio programs in your car. My bet is once you see the results, you'll listen to them all the time.

Audio programs are more available now than ever with podcasts and downloadable books you can access right from your smartphone. Many cars come with jacks you can plug your phone or other devices into. You can have a library in your car! Now, that's amazing!

- **Grow together as a family.**

Another great way to find net time is to incorporate personal development into your relationship and family time. This benefits you in multiple ways. Having a rock-solid foundation to build your marriage or partnership upon will put you miles ahead of the masses.

My family and I enjoy going online and choosing books to read together. We often read to one another, sharing favorite passages once a day and discussing the principles of success or other ideas we're exploring, and the progress we're making toward our goals.

We set up a family Facebook group and share quotes and passages that move us, and each other, to greatness.

Leaders are Learners.

Two things that will most dramatically shape your life are what you read and the people you associate with.

Working hard is not enough. My parents worked hard their entire lives and had nothing to show for it at the end.

You must continue to learn. You must continue to grow. The world is changing at a record speed, and you're either keeping up or falling behind.

Happiness is not a destination; it's a process. It's a process of growing out of the shell of who you are and evolving into the person you can become.

All of us have addictions (in one form or another), so you might as well become addicted to learning and growing. Reading and developing yourself will ensure you're happier, healthier, and more appreciative of the moments making up your day.

I hope I've removed many of your, "I don't know where to start," obstacles and given you some ideas to illuminate your path.

Now, it's up to you.

Three Things to Act on

Before completing the next step, look in a mirror and say: "I understand success comes from the implementation of knowledge, not the acquisition of it; therefore, I choose to step into an epic life by taking action on my new-found knowledge. As I read, I will capture the ideas that resonate with me and apply them to my life until I master them. Period. This is what badasses do, and I'm a badass. The result of these committed actions is an epic life!"

Action Step

- **Based on what you learned in this chapter, record three things in your journal or below that you're committed to**

acting on. Take as much space as you need to outline not only what you'll act upon, but how (steps you'll take), and the all-important why (your reason and result motivations and expectations). Write:

I commit to take action on:

_____

_____

_____

_____

_____

_____

_____

I commit to take action on:

_____

_____

_____

_____

_____

_____

_____

I commit to take action on:

_____

_____

_____

_____

_____

_____

_____

_____

CHAPTER ONE RECAP

➢ Schedule at least thirty minutes a day for personal development and study. (I highly recommend the book *The Miracle Morning* by my friend, Hal Elrod). If you want to get through this process more rapidly, do more than thirty minutes. If thirty minutes is all you can spare, that's a great place to start.

➢ Find "net time", downtime you can easily replace with personal development, like time spent in the car, standing in lines, or watching TV. Read books with your family, and turn family time or date night into "growth" time.

➢ Pay attention to your self-talk, and take steps to eliminate the negative from your thoughts. Catch words like "wish", "can't", "I don't have time", and eliminate them from your vocabulary. Even a seemingly positive word like "hope" can be upgraded (more on that later).

➢ Because thoughts are things that lead to actions, which lead to results, if you don't change the seeds (your inputs) that create your garden (your results), you're going to continue to produce the same fruits repeatedly, quite possibly lemons.

➢ If you're reading this book, you're already sowing the seeds for a new harvest with exciting new results. Pat yourself on the back. Good job!

➢ Now, pick up your journal (or record below) the amount of time per day you'll dedicate to your reprograming and personal development.

_____

CHAPTER TWO PREVIEW

A ship with no goal will stop at any port of call.
How would you like to attract whatever you want
efficiently and effectively? Rule number two will
give you clarity and confidence along with a
simple process you can use again and again
to sharpen your focus and achieve
specific, astonishing results.

CHAPTER TWO

"A man with no imagination has no wings."
Mohammad Ali

We're all familiar with the concept of setting goals, but many people tell me they don't have a system for setting goals or they aren't fully utilizing the power of goal setting.

Let's talk about goals in general before diving into the best way to harness the power of goal setting.

First, what's a goal?

A goal is a specific, desired result or outcome within a given time. Perhaps you want a new car, a promotion, or a vacation.

For a long time, one of my goals was to shoot under seventy in golf. For years, I had that dream until I got serious, set a goal, and achieved it. Twenty years after starting golf, I shot a sixty-nine, not once but three times in the same year!

In my book *The Power of Your Identity*, I explain why (once I shot a sixty-nine) it was easy to do it again. I'm still playing the best golf of my life, recently beating my own goal by shooting a sixty-eight!

It's never too late to achieve a dream or cause your character to grow.

When I shot sixty-eight, did I get a trophy? No! I got so much more. Satisfaction. Pride. The sense of achievement that only comes when you set a goal, work for it, and get there.

There is something magic that happens inside when you achieve your goals. It's this feeling (whatever it is for you) you're after. Setting goals becomes easier and more fun when you focus on this amazing feeling and the emotions that come with achieving our goals.

For me, pride when others respected me was what I was after. If I shot my dream score, people would talk about how exceptional I was. Recognition would make me feel important, unique, and wanted. Feelings missing in my childhood.

Growing up, I didn't fit in. Even as an adult, what I wanted most from my sixty-nine game was a well-earned feeling of pride. Focusing on how great I would feel when I succeeded fueled my efforts to hit my goal and then exceed it.

If I hadn't thought about the real reason I wanted to reach my golf goal, I would've been chasing a number that seemed impossible to achieve.

When you set goals, always understand the emotions behind them. This will give you clarity.

At times, you'll gain feelings you desire in the process of achieving your goal. I'm proud of myself whenever I put in the work required to hit a goal in any area of my life.

You might not need to reach a goal to gain the feelings you seek. You could experience the feelings you desire just by trying. Or you could find new directions to explore once you begin. This is exciting! Suddenly, you might change course and set new goals. With clarity comes exhilaration. Fear disappears as you head off confidently in a new direction.

Without a well-defined goal, it's easy to get distracted. Bored. Frustrated. You never arrive at your destination because you're not headed anywhere in particular.

If you don't know where you're going, then any road might take you there or lead you off into the woods. Lost. Without direction and focus, it's easy to give up and turn back. Even if you're on a good path, how would you know? Soon, you stop trying.

When I coach people, I often start by asking them what they want.

Most people answer by telling me what they don't want. They're stuck attracting more of what they don't want because that's all they focus on.

So, that's where we start. By learning to focus on what you want.

RAS

Do you know what you want? Are you employing your RAS (reticular activating system) to help you, or are you living in Hopium (a place of hope and fantasy where dreams are wished for but never come true)?

Many people think hoping or wishing is the same as goal setting, but this is too vague. So blurry you can't get fired-up about making it happen. You don't know where to start.

When your goals are unclear, you see a shiny object and you go off course. You're easily distracted. If there's turbulence or resistance on the path toward your uncertain goal, you stop. Maybe you start again, and something else catches your eye. Ultimately, the path toward your goal ends up being a loop, back and forth, around and around. Before you know it, you're exhausted! It becomes easier to make up excuses about why you failed than to continue pursuing your goal.

You construct a story. Blame enters the room. Criticizing and justifying take over your thoughts and your focus. You become disempowered, and you quit.

Do you relate to these patterns? Does this behavior happen to everyone? Yes. When we don't have a plan or clear reasons backed by excitement and determination to push us forward.

Can you overcome old patterns or self-defeating behavior? Yes! When your goals are etched in your mind, emblazoned across your desktop, written down and reviewed in your journal or in this book, on your calendar, and dream board, written on sticky notes stuck on your mirrors, and you follow a system for tracking your goals (developed after clearly identifying your desired results), your chances of achieving your goals go up substantially.

What you measure improves. What you measure and report on

improves exponentially!

Successful people have a sense of direction and purpose. They stay committed no matter what happens around them. Clearly defined goals help them do this.

Research shows 97% of people don't set goals. Yet, the 3% of goal setters possess 97% of the world's wealth! Is there a correlation? Of course, there is! Goal setting is directly connected with success.

Why don't more people set goals? The reason is simple. Think about it. Have you ever set a goal and put an incredible amount of effort, passion, and energy into achieving it only to fail, and watch your efforts fade away to nothing? Have you ever experienced humiliation or embarrassment over not reaching a goal you set for yourself? Experiences like those usually force you to into "story mode"—justifying or criticizing, or blaming external factors. This is your brain's way of protecting you from perceived danger and bad feelings. You develop momentum for why not to try again instead of reasons why you'll achieve your goal if you keep pushing. Your story makes it easy to quit. You take the easy way out, and listen to your brain shrieking at you that it's safer not to try again. And you're left feeling the pain of failure.

Pain is a powerful force. Left unguided, it will rob you of your will to pursue tomorrow's goals.

In chapter nine, I'll teach you how to re-frame events, so you don't lose your drive when you hit extreme emotional moments. For now, know it's possible with new tools to tear past your goal resistance and fear of failure.

RRAFT (Result, Reason, Action, Feedback, and Thrill)

RRAFT—the goal setting process I developed—transformed my life. You can experience this transformation too.

Goals equal life fuel. Goals equal energy, passion, direction, charisma, excitement, mission, and purpose. They define the things that make you feel alive, fulfilled, and on purpose.

Do you want to feel on purpose? Do you want to make a difference in the world? Do you want to feel as though you're growing and improving?

The most successful people I know get a lot of satisfaction and happiness out of growing and improving any area of their lives, whether it's their health, their waist size, their golf score, or their bank account.

Think about the happiest moments in your life. When they happened, were you experiencing progress and knocking out goals left and right? Were you achieving dreams or working toward them?

If that's all it takes, why not schedule goals and actions, and start being happy today and along the way?

Put your previous experience with goals and goal setting out of your mind as you begin using RRAFT to help direct your focus and clearly define where you're going, so you can remain open to this powerful five-step process.

First, think about one of your top goals, one you're passionate about. It may be one that's been on the back burner. It may be one you've given up on because it seemed impossible to achieve. It may be one you think about a lot but never attempt. Pull it to the surface, dust it off, write it down in your journal or below, and get it ready because you're going to RRAFT it.

Grab a pencil, and write the following and their answers. Do this right now.

My top goal:

_____

_____

_____

Deadline for achieving my goal (year, month, day, time):

_____

_____

_____

Now, write the **result** you want, **the first R in RRAFT**. Be specific, and put it within a timeline.

If you want to purchase a new car, don't write "I want a new car". Write "I will purchase a brand new, Melbourne Red Metallic BMW Z4 by month, day, year, and even the time (2:00 PM)". By clearly defining your goal, you create an image in your mind and provide a deadline to help define your target. In the process of considering your goal, you should research how much your new car will cost and break that down by whatever timeframe you're working with.

_____

_____

_____

_____

_____

Surround yourself with pictures of your car. Put pictures in your workspace, on your phone, screen savers, and dream board. Put one in your Epic Life Blueprint journal, or use it as a bookmark as you read this book. The more you visualize your new car, the better.

Why does showing your mind what's important to you work so well?

Earlier, I mentioned your RAS (reticular activating system). This part of your brain, once given a target and information, goes to work finding resources to make your goals reality.

Your mind monitors thousands of bits of information constantly.

Your heart beat, your thoughts, your wishes, and fears. Once you send a request to your mind, asking it to focus and look for something specific (let's say you're getting married), like a scavenger hunter, your mind starts pointing out items about honeymoons, wedding dresses, ads on TV about diamonds, and other things relating to weddings seem to pop up all the time.

Were these wedding things there before? Yes. But you didn't tell your brain to find them. So, it focused on what it was asked to focus on or whatever it felt like thinking about.

What happens when you don't ask your mind to focus on anything, and you don't set goals? Your mind is open to suggestions. Free to wander. Your mind never stops working.

You know the inner voice that keeps talking to you? It makes a great employee if you give it a game plan. However, it's easily distracted if you allow everyone else to employ your mind. It will meander and focus on its primary concern—keeping you safe.

Advertisers are hyper-aware most people don't set goals or know what they want. So, they put your mind (your employee) to work for them. They suggest you need to buy a beer, or go on a vacation, see a movie, or take a pill to feel better.

Have you ever experienced pain and found yourself in the pharmacy thinking you should buy Advil or Tylenol to relieve it? Whose voice is telling you to do this? The advertisers. This compulsion was planted there by someone you allowed to employ your staff for free to get what they want. This is huge!

Left undirected, your mind will go work for someone else's objectives, making their dreams come true, not yours. I can't think of a better reason to take control of your thoughts, and direct them toward goals you want to achieve.

Let's get started. Open your journal and write the following and your answer(s), or record them in this book:

My goal(s)/result(s) =

The second R in RRAFT stands for reasons. This is the all-important "why" behind your goal and one of the most powerful forces in the RRAFT process.

When the reasons behind your goals are so compelling, vivid, and real to you; when they give you shivers, and keep you up with excitement, you're less likely to give up before achieving your goals.

One of the major reasons people don't achieve their goals is because they're unclear about why they're important in the first place.

Clarity leads to power.

Action Steps

- **Take sixty seconds, and write as many benefits and reasons for achieving your goal that you can. Write the first reasons that come to mind, and go with those. Let your imagination run wild.**

  Describe what it will feel like owning your new BMW. What it will feel like to drive it. How it will sound, smell, and feel when you walk out to the garage and see it sitting there waiting for you. Don't edit the process. Just write (for one minute), as fast as you can, all the reasons why you want the object or achievement you desire. Go! Go! Go! Now.

_____

_____

_____

_____

_____

_____

_____

_____

_____

_____

_____

_____

_____

- **Next, spend a second minute writing what it will cost you and what it will feel like if you don't achieve your goal. Be clear, be specific, and don't edit. Just write.**

_____

_____

_____

_____

_____

_____

_____

_____

_____

_____

_____

_____

_____

_____

_____

_____

_____

Keep in mind you can always come back to this part of the process later to add additional thoughts as they come up. Writing down your goals is not a static process to be done and then filed away. Review them frequently. Tweak them. Change the reasons behind them.

Action Step

- **Use your journal to answer these questions, or record them here:**

  What will it cost me if I don't achieve my goal? How will I feel if I don't achieve my goal?

_____

_____

_____

_____

_____

_____

_____

_____

_____

_____

_____

_____

_____

_____

_____

_____

_____

_____

_____

_____

The next step (the "A" in RRAFT) is actions. This is your to-do list, broken down into annual, quarterly, monthly, weekly, and daily steps you'll take.

Weekly and monthly benchmarks are good timelines because they are small enough to put things into a manageable perspective and large enough to make a measurable impact on your overall result.

Record tasks in your journal, or in this book, and on whatever tool you use to organize your daily schedule. If you don't have a tool for this, get one. Use a Day-Timer, or your Outlook program, or an app (I like Wunderlist). Write your daily to-do list, and track your action items, or you won't complete them. Do the most important tasks first, and don't move to the second group until the first is completed. Use the power of focus.

Action Step

- **Use your journal, this book, or another tool to create a list of steps required to achieve your goal.**

_____

_____

_____

_____

_____

_____

_____

_____

_____

_____

_____

The forth step (the "F" in RRAFT) is feedback, one of my favorites. Feedback is nothing more than information. It's not good or bad.

It's not right or wrong. It's raw data that can be used to determine if we're being effective or not. Feedback is a way of measuring your actions to determine if they're working or not.

Suppose you make 100 sales calls this week, and they result in ten sales. A ratio appears. Now, you can predict the future. If your goal is to lose ten pounds this month, the scale provides immediate feedback, information to help you move closer to your goal.

Things are things, situations are moments in time, and all of it has no good or bad attached to it until you make it so. So, don't get discouraged or disappointed.

Say, "This is the feedback. Either my actions are working or they're not." Now, you can apply energy in the right direction or celebrate your success.

Once you've completed some action items, record feedback in your journal or in the space below. Adjust your timing or action plan based on what you've learned (but don't fall into the trap of making excuses or quitting if you're falling short in some areas).

Action Step

- **Use your journal to answer these questions, or record them here:**

What worked? What didn't? How can I improve?

_____

_____

_____

_____

_____

_____

_____

_____

_____

_____

_____

_____

_____

_____

_____

_____

_____

_____

_____

To make the most effective use of feedback, it's important to record it, and break it down in a way designed to move you forward, not drag you down.

CSI

Creative suggestions for improvement (CSI) are invaluable tools. Everything you learn as you progress can be used to improve results and propel you more effectively toward your goals.

I do this anytime I experience something significant, whether it's playing golf, or leading a seminar, or handling a difficult moment with a friend. To pull the learning from the experience, I CSI it.

Here's how to do it:

Step one is to ask yourself this question: What worked? Be specific. Examine your emotions and outcomes. Focus on the positive or enjoyable. Validate your successes. Celebrate them.

Step two is to ask yourself what didn't work. The goal is to take note of patterns. If every time you play golf, you notice the ball is going to the right, you can take steps to correct the issue and see faster results. You can break previously held patterns of behavior, and develop new and better ones.

Step three is to ask others for feedback. Sometimes, we have a hard time seeing the full picture, especially during difficult situations. Talk with people who've gone through the experience with you. Ask what you could improve and what worked.

Sometimes, we all need to know somebody else believes in us. You may tend to stack all your mistakes into a big pile, so you can't see the possibilities or examine them with an impartial eye. This is negative programing that will move you farther away from success. Being open to finding the good in mistakes or setbacks is a skill all winners employ. Asking for, and listening to, feedback from others is vitally important for this reason. Get another perspective whenever you can, especially from people getting the results you desire.

When I started in real estate, I was a complete failure. I grew frustrated, working with buyers and driving around town seven days a week, showing people home after home without a sale. I was too shy to ask for feedback, so the only feedback I got was from the market (which is a great teacher; however, it's also the slowest teacher as you must try everything on your own). By asking others, you leverage their mistakes. But I hadn't learned that yet. Each showing seemed to take longer and longer. I fell behind on my appointments. I worried about not getting paid for my hard work. I started skipping lunch because I was too busy to take a break. I wasn't examining my results using the CSI process. My only feedback came from my mind which told me I couldn't be a successful realtor. I became angry. I blamed the circumstances and the environment. I didn't take responsibility for my behavior. My response to all this pressure created such angst in my body that I started to express my frustration in the office.

One day, I was cursing at the photocopy machine when the top agent, Nicole, said, "I know what you're going through. I felt like you do when I started out too, but you'll get over it. I know it's painful. One day, Rock, you're going to be the top agent in this company. I know it."

I didn't believe her.

Then she told me, "I see it in you. I see you go out time and time again. I see your determination and the way you work longer hours than anyone else even though you aren't getting results yet. You have what it takes."

This was a turning point for me. Somebody believed in me. Somebody felt I could do something I thought I couldn't.

I kept plugging away and moving forward. A few years later, I became the top agent in the office, and the next year, I bought the entire office.

Nicole was right. I did have what it took. Her belief in me helped me see the potential in myself.

When you receive good feedback from a respected source, it empowers you and increases your self-belief. This is known as "social proof".

Since those early days, I created a tribe of people who encourage each other to achieve greatness. Visit M1 to join because if you're not part of a tribe that stands up for you, believes in you, and cheers you on, you're missing a key success ingredient.

Using the CSI process, you'll reward yourself for successful behavior and rapidly eliminate things that aren't serving you.

Finally, in the RRAFT system, we have "T" for thrills. Thrills are celebrations when you achieve your goal, but more importantly, they're celebrations of little victories along the way.

Make sure to build in thrills at the end of each day, week, and month. If you said you'd make ten calls today, or send out ten post-cards, or sell one unit of your product, and you do these things, make sure to celebrate your accomplishments when you achieve them.

This is an important part of programing ourselves. Celebrations let your mind know you appreciate your efforts to get what you want in life. Otherwise, you risk feeling like the goal posts keep moving. Achieve and work, achieve and work. The cycle never ends. That's a negative message you don't want to embrace. If you do, you risk associating only hard work with your efforts and become demotivated.

Celebrate while each small push forward is fresh in your mind and relevant to the timeframe at hand. This is a powerful part of the CSI process too. Never fail to look for things you can celebrate, no matter how small your accomplishment might seem in the grand scheme of things.

When you find something to celebrate, write it in your journal, on your calendar, or in this book. Review these accomplishments regularly to reinforce your progress and the good feelings that come with them.

Action Step

- **Use your journal to answer these questions, or record them here:**

    How did I celebrate milestones on the way to achieving my goal? How will I celebrate next time?

_____

_____

_____

It's important to review your goals regularly. I recommend you do this at least once a week as you're creating your following week's schedule and action plan. Sunday night is a good time for many people. Others prefer to do this Friday night to end their week. Whatever works best for you is fine. The key is committing to spending at least ten minutes reviewing your goals each week and following through.

This system of "reverse engineering" your week will make you exceptionally efficient and productive, so you'll achieve more. Record and add goals and action plans to whatever system you're using.

Now that you have a clear picture of the RRAFT process and how it works, don't overcomplicate it. Keep it simple.

Be specific, and spend most of your time thinking about the underlying reasons why you're committed to reaching your goals. Once you commit your objectives to paper, and you're crystal clear about them, your reticular activating system will kick-in and focus on your objective. If you want a red BMW, you'll start seeing red BMWs everywhere. It happens with everything we turn our attention and focus to.

At the same time, the intangible power of the universe will begin handing you answers. People will show up in your life to help, and all the pieces will fall into place. The universe will magically conspire to help you achieve your goals.

Three Things to Act on

Before completing the next step, look in a mirror and say: "I understand success comes from the implementation of knowledge, not the acquisition of it; therefore, I choose to step into an epic life by taking action on my new-found knowledge. As I read, I will capture the ideas that resonate with me and apply them to my life until I master them. Period. This is what badasses do, and I'm a badass. The result of these committed actions is an epic life!"

Action Step

- **Based on what you learned in this chapter, record three things in your journal or below that you're committed to acting on. Take as much space as you need to outline not only what you'll act upon, but how (steps you'll take), and the all-important why (your reason and result motivations and expectations). Write:**

I commit to take action on:

_____

_____

_____

_____

_____

_____

_____

_____

_____

I commit to take action on:

_____

_____

_____

_____

_____

_____

_____

_____

_____

I commit to take action on:

_____

_____

_____

_____

_____

_____

_____

_____

CHAPTER TWO RECAP

➤ Most of our fears, stresses and excuses revolve around our thoughts, perceptions, and self-imposed limitations (past pro-graming). My mentor and teacher, Anandagiri, from One World Academy in India says, "We have an irresistible temptation to hold onto the negative."

➤ Every time we set a goal and don't achieve it, we risk being disappointed. Often, the way we deal with disappointment is to play the victim. Examine your patterns to avoid creating a negative identity.

➤ Pay attention to your self-talk, and take steps to eliminate the negative from your thoughts. Focus on positive motivations for each of your goals. Meditation is a great method for removing the habit of holding onto the negative, helping you focus on the positive instead.

➤ RRAFT your goals. Complete the exercises in chapter one and two if you skipped them. And stop skipping exercises.

➤ Review your goals, update your reasons for them if necessary, and record your progress, feedback, and needed adjustments each week.

➤ Celebrate all progress.

Notes

CHAPTER THREE PREVIEW

Discover your special gifts and talents,
and learn to focus your energy to maximize them.
Rule number three will help you work smarter
and achieve your goals faster while
being more fulfilled.

CHAPTER THREE

Rule Three: Exploit your gifts, and sharpen
your skills.

"Your talent is your multiplier.
The more energy you invest in it, the greater the yield."
Marcus Buckingham

This rule, exploiting your natural gifts, could change your life. Let's begin by exploring gifts and identifying exactly what I mean by "gifts".

Monique McDonald, an expert at identifying individuals' strengths, says there are twenty-four possible gifts available to you within the cards you've been dealt in life. When you're born, you'll probably receive four to six of these gifts. They'll range anywhere from artisanship, to musical talent, to athletic ability. You might also have the gift of hospitality if you like to take care of other people. Maybe you have the gift of compassion like Mother Teresa.

When you use your natural gifts, not only do other people light up around you and experience great joy, you experience an incredible sense of fulfillment and energy. When you live your gifts, and do what you love, your energy goes up. Time seems to disappear.

Action Step

- **Go through the following list of twenty-four possible gifts and identify the ones that resonate strongest within you.**

Record them in your journal, or mark them here.

Assistance/Helping
Compassion/Mercy
Craftsmanship
Cultural Integration
Encouragement
Extraordinary Trust
Facilitation
Foresight
Giving
Healing
Hospitality
Intercession
Knowledge
Leadership
Music
Planning/Coordination
Service
Simplicity
Singleness
Spiritual Challenge
Spiritual Sensitivity
Teaching
Wisdom
Writing

Sales professionals, great negotiators, decision makers, or people with extra-positive attitudes were not born with those skills. They cultivated them, and you can too. Knowing yourself is crucial to maximizing your efforts.

If you're leading a company and have not read the book *Rocket Fuel*, I highly recommend it to learn if you're a visionary (22% of the population) or an integrator (less than 6% of the population).

Napoleon Hill, author of *Think and Grow Rich*, says there are approximately seventeen characteristics all highly successful people have. Mr. Hill discovered this after spending twenty-five years researching and interviewing some of the most successful people of the time. He learned these characteristics are cultivated. Highly successful people had learned how to be great negotiators, sales professionals, influencers of people, and decision makers. People were not just born with a positive mental attitude; they cultivated a positive mental attitude.

What are you doing to cultivate your attitude? Now might be a good time to look at what you've added to your daily routine to grow your positivity.

Many people say they've been dealt a bad hand. They cannot succeed. They feel as if they're not talented, lucky, or fortunate enough. The cards are stacked against them. But you have an opportunity to make huge strides in a positive direction by understanding all successful people start by doing what they love and cultivating their gifts in the areas of their strengths. They recognize everyone has some skills that come easily and naturally, and they maximize these skills first.

Many of us ignore our callings or fail to follow our hearts out of fear or perceived obligation to others. They struggle through life trying to develop gifts that don't come naturally to them while failing to maximize their real talents. They do what they can to make a living rather than developing their talents (gifts) over time and living a happy, fulfilling life.

Action Steps

- **List your top five gifts from the previous list in your journal or here.**

_____

_____

_____

- **Use your journal to write and answer this question, or record your answer here:**

  How will I use my strengths to help others or fulfill a need?

_____

_____

_____

_____

_____

_____

_____

_____

_____

In his groundbreaking book *Outliers*, Malcolm Gladwell says if you want to become great at something (what he calls a genius level), all you must do is commit 10,000 hours of dedicated practice to that skill. It could be playing the violin or becoming a chess master. It might be mastering a sport, cooking, or fixing computers. Gladwell determined when you spend 10,000 hours developing a skill—any skill—in an area you're passionate about, you'll become a master of it. You'll be able to do it in your sleep.

We all have this ability in some areas of our lives, guaranteed. Sadly, many people never acknowledge it.

Think about some of the basics you've mastered over the years— driving a car, brushing your teeth, putting on your clothes. These are simple examples, but appreciate the fact that you have hit the mastery level in these areas. You can do them without even thinking anymore. You've put in 10,000 hours learning these rudimentary skills.

What if you knew you could succeed at anything you desire if you do it with focus, planning, and put in 10,000 hours? Wouldn't you commit to doing it? Wouldn't you make time?

Some people make what they do look easy, like artists and athletes. It's as if they're successful because they were born with a special gift others don't have. But they're exploiting their gift after consciously developing these skills.

The average football player practices 100 hours for every hour they play in a real game. They can run the same pattern repeatedly and can execute so well because they've invested so much time practicing. After a while, their body and their neurology reacts without hesitation because of repetition and habit. They've honed their natural abilities and focused their efforts on developing them.

What if you were that committed to a craft or a passion? Where could that passion take you? Are you that committed?

I was a terrible public speaker, but through practice and coaching, I now command the stage with confidence, and I impact many lives. Who would have thought a skinny little farm kid his brother and sisters laughed at for not being able to talk properly, who was not good in school, and dyslectic, would ever get to that level of public speaking?

There are no shortcuts. If you want to improve, you're going to have to zero in on the skills you want to develop and practice, practice, practice. Throughout our lives, we've been taught practice makes perfect. But what practice really does is make permanent. Repeat a skill or behavior and it becomes permanent, whether it's a good habit or a bad one.

In the past, you may have unconsciously practiced skills of failure. If you want to live a life of easy success, you'll need to consciously choose to practice skills that build your inner character.

"I fell in love with repetition," says Jeff Rouse, Olympic champion and backstroke world-record holder for nine years.

Fall in love with your habits. Make them well planned, and doable, and stick to them. Find role models like Jeff. Learn from them.

As I mentioned earlier, one of the best ways to become successful is to find a coach or a mentor achieving the results you desire. Identify the habits that created their success. Think the way they think. Do what they do. Make their habits and guiding principles your habits and guiding principles, and your blueprint will gain an additional level of clarity.

Action Step

- **Use your journal to write the names of two people who inspire you and are successful in the areas you wish to succeed in, or write them here.**

_____

_____

_____

Study them, search online and research the habits they say led to their success. Contact them via email or through social media, and ask them for specific advice. Most people are more than happy to share the disciplines they've employed to achieve their dreams. It's a huge jolt of positive energy to connect with someone who inspires you.

It's important to remember that it doesn't have to be all or nothing. You don't have to be a master of everything! A good level of competence is all you need to move within the right circles.

For instance, I'm not very musically or rhythmically inclined. However, I took dancing lessons because I felt it could be a great value socially to be able to dance. I took some very intense dancing lessons that were not a lot of fun at the time, but I got over the initial hurdles and rough stages to a point where I could do some basic moves. Now, I don't claim to be a dance master, but I'm pretty good, and I've developed a level of confidence to step onto the dance floor instead of being stuck in my chair, watching others have fun and wishing I could do the same. I'm not gifted, but I became skilled.

Studies show the biggest regret humans have the older they get is the risks they didn't take.

Developing a skill is the antidote to regret. Learning means progress.

Tony Robbins often says progress is akin to happiness, so building your skills will make you happier and less regretful later in life.

What are you waiting for? By now, you should have a good idea of changes you'd like to make in your life. Get to it!

I used to work at a training company, warming up the audience before a seminar. We used music, and there was a lot of clapping involved. I was a nervous wreck the first time I had to do this. My timing with clapping is not great (that rhythm thing again) and having to clap to the music at the right time, in front of hundreds of people, freaked me out! But I became skilled at it over time, through practice, and before long, I was genuinely excited getting out there on stage and clapping my heart out.

Take a minute to think about skills you'd like to develop. Dream big! Think of something you love, something you could spend the rest of your life doing happily. What benefits would there be for you if you developed these skills? Would focusing on them enhance your character or your profession? Imagine how cool it would be doing these things.

Action Step

- **Use your journal to write three skills you'd like to develop, or record them here.**

_____

_____

_____

Oprah Winfrey, Martha Stewart, Tiger Woods, Wayne Gretzky, Tony Robbins, and many other talented individuals paid the price of those 10,000 hours.

The best part about developing your natural skills and exploiting your gifts is that you probably have done much of the work already.

Many people think 10,000 hours is beyond their reach or too difficult to even imagine. When you consider how much time you've already put into your gifted areas, you'll realize you simply need a bit of focus to get you over the hump to above average.

One of the big challenges with developing our strengths is our limiting beliefs and tendency to follow the path of least resistance. We do what's easy. We do what's convenient. We do what we think other people expect us to do. After we finish school, we take a job or an opportunity to do something because it's familiar, or it's the first thing that comes along. The next thing you know, we have a mortgage, a car, and kids. We find it hard to go back and pursue our dreams.

In a landmark study of 1,500 people, 1,275 chose a career because of money. The other 225 people chose a career based on their passion, gifts, and things that lit them up inside. Several years later, of the original 1,500 people, 101 millionaires had been created. Can you guess how many millionaires came from each group? Of the 225 people who pursued their passion or their gifts, almost 50% of them became millionaires (the entire 101!). Of the other, much larger, group that pursued money, not one of them went on to become a millionaire. Not one!

When you follow your passion, exploit your gifts, and do what you love, money, inner-wealth, and success will follow.

People with passion rarely use the word work. Without passion, one is reduced to a life of mediocrity and indifference. When you're passionate, you're focused, purposeful, and determined, without having to try.

A word of caution about working with your gifts—in *The E Myth*, Michael Gerber claims the mistake made by most entrepreneurs is taking a gift they have and trying to run a business with it. For example, if a chef wants to run a restaurant, only to find out the skills of managing people, negotiating leases, credit, purchasing inventory, accounting, and running the business are all skills they don't have, they'll probably fail. Since these are not areas of interest for them, they don't invest the time necessary to develop the skills nor do they have the resources to outsource them. They wind up struggling or going out of business, bankrupt. If they do manage to stay in business, they go through their career frustrated and unhappy because it's nearly impossible to be good at everything, and doing things that are not your gifts will drain you of energy.

Just because you have a gift doesn't mean you should go into business unless you're willing to develop the skills and line up resources to support it. Do what you love, but choose wisely. Use your skills in areas where they'll do you the most good, and outsource the rest. Work smarter, and barter whenever possible.

I have a "don't do list" I purposefully built. My team is grateful for it. I'm lousy with paperwork and lose papers often as I don't get excited by details. Now, I have people on my team who get to shine handling the details.

Your lack in one area is someone else's gift and opportunity to shine. Don't rob others of their gifts. Identify yours and exploit them. Surround yourself with people who compliment you, and celebrate them by letting them exploit their talents.

Three Things to Act on

Before completing the next step, look in a mirror and say: "I understand success comes from the implementation of knowledge, not the acquisition of it; therefore, I choose to step into an epic life by taking action on my new-found knowledge. As I read, I will capture the ideas that resonate with me and apply them to my life until I master them. Period. This is what badasses do, and I'm a badass. The result of these committed actions is an epic life!"

Action Step

- **Based on what you learned in this chapter, record three things in your journal or below that you're committed to acting on. Take as much space as you need to outline not only what you'll act upon, but how (steps you'll take), and the all-important why (your reason and result motivatio- and expectations). Write:**

I commit to take action on:

_____

_____

_____

_____

_____

_____

_____

_____

_____

I commit to take action on:

_____

_____

_____

_____

_____

_____

_____

_____

_____

I commit to take action on:

_____

_____

_____

_____

_____

_____

_____

_____

CHAPTER THREE RECAP

> Cultivate the gifts you were born with before attempting to develop skills in an area where you're very unfamiliar.

> Maximizing your strengths is easier, more fun, builds confidence, and will allow you to participate in circles with people who can help you grow and further your cause.

> According to Malcolm Gladwell (in his book *Outliers*), it takes 10,000 hours to master a skill. So, don't get discouraged until you have put in the time. Your breakthrough may happen later in the 10,000-hour sequence. Be patient. Be persistent.

> Practice makes permanent, not perfect.

> Exploiting your gifts is likely to be a service to someone else's needs. Barter and exchange your abilities for services you need but lack the proper skills or desire to learn.

> Make a "don't do" list. Allow others to shine, and reduce tasks that sap your energy.

Notes

CHAPTER FOUR PREVIEW

In chapter four, you'll discover how you can find the passion and motivation to develop your skills even when they're things you don't really love.

CHAPTER FOUR

"Every man dies. Not every man really lives."
William Wallace

This may be the most powerful rule of all of them. Like strapping on a jetpack to access the driving force inside you that will cause you to take more action than you ever have before. It's going to give you some leverage and a winning edge to help you act despite your fear, doubt, worry, frustration, sadness, or disappointment. Maybe you've tried hard before, and you've lost faith that things will work out. Well, those days are over!

In this chapter, we'll explore your motivational hot buttons, and learn to take action despite your fears.

First, ask yourself what you want to feel. Do you want to feel special or cherished? Excited? How about happy? Do you want to feel a sense of challenge, determination, or drive? A desire to connect or feel a genuine sense of freedom? Do you want to be in control, confident, charismatic, or develop an extremely high level of self-esteem?

Before you can work on your hot buttons, you need to discover what drives you, not what you *think* should drive you, but what really drives you.

Maslow's hierarchy of needs outlines the fundamental emotional requirements all humans need to survive, from the most basic to the more advanced. Tony Robbins pulled from this list to come up with his own. I've combined the two to form my interpretation of the path to motivation based on our needs.

Comfort Zone

Your comfort zone is your calm happy place of smooth sailing and no worries where you avoid pain, and enjoy as much pleasure as possible. If something disturbs your comfort zone—you lose your job, your passport on a business trip, or you miss a big meeting—you'll be out of your comfort zone, and you'll have trouble focusing on other areas of your life. Your marriage, your family, your passions, hobbies, and other pleasurable pursuits will suffer because you're out of your comfort zone.

Your brain works 24/7 keeping you alive and safe. I'm grateful for this. Otherwise, we might die at a much younger age. But many people become victims of the fear our minds employ to keep us in our comfort zones. Many people resort to drugs and alcohol to override the mind from keeping us fearful of things that are not life-threatening.

What does this all mean? We keep talking about how our brains over use adrenaline to scare us into not doing things or to activate the fight or flight mechanics to keep us safe. Unless you consciously override the quantities of chemicals unleashed in your nervous system, it's easy to mistake being late for a meeting or losing your keys as something awful enough to need a dose of chemicals like we'd get if we had to run away from a sabretooth tiger. The effect of this overdose of unnecessary chemicals is stress, burn out, fatigue, high blood pressure, and much more. I'll give you the antidote to this later. For now, just understand your system needs an upgrade.

Variety and Uncertainty

People who need variety and uncertainty like to try different things, from sky diving to scuba diving. They are happy to try new restaurants or drive a different route home.

I like to move my place of residence often, play different sports, and travel to unexplored countries. I prefer uncertainty and variety. Boredom, or the possibility of experiencing boredom, is a prime motivator for me to take action. Knowing this, I make sure I have a list of positive things to choose from to keep myself engaged.

Others are driven to experience a more consistent level of comfort and security. They've had the same job for thirty years, live in the same house their entire lives, drive the same car made by the same manufacturer, and always eat the same food at the same restaurant.

Some people have a higher need for consistency and prefer to live within their comfort zones.

Since there's no right or wrong here, be honest about who you are and how you're wired. Avoid looking closely at yourself with judgments about the type of person you "should" be or would like to be. For now, just figure out who you are.

When you understand your wiring, and embrace yourself for who you really are, you'll achieve so much more, activated by your newfound passion and understanding.

I grew up on a farm and was raised surrounded by uncertainty in some ways and routine in others. My parents were rarely around. Starting when I was very young, I was responsible for feeding horses, making my own lunches, and countless other chores. I left home at seventeen to travel the world. I needed adventure. Craved a change. A lack of routine.

You might crave the opposite, but generally, you'll be happiest living like you grew up. The person who grew up in the Bronx or in the streets will likely crave more uncertainty than the person who grew up in a suburb with a dog, parents who were home consistently, and a stable life.

Community and Connection

Are you part of an association or a group? How about a church? At work, are you a member of a peer group that goes to lunch or shopping together? Are you into sports, or are you part of a professional or amateur team, playing every weekend with the same team members? If so, you probably have a strong need for a sense of community and belonging.

To some degree, most of us have a strong desire to be part of things, connected to those around us. Therefore, at an event like a hockey game or a baseball game, it's always more exciting when the stadium is full, and the crowd is screaming. The sense of community and connection with other like-minded people enhances your overall experience. It magnifies it, making it that much more delicious.

When I accomplish something, one of the first things I want to do is share and celebrate it with other people.

Almost all suffering comes from a sense of separateness and the feeling of not being connected. You can connect with God, nature, food, and even your problems. You just need to decide what's most important to you.

Personal Importance

You might love being called unique or different. You might enjoy shocking people and defying the odds. You always find a way to stand out. Or you like to blend in. You do all you can to deflect attention away from yourself.

My son ranks personal importance as a huge motivator for him. He's in great physical shape and is often asked to show off his body. He has an eight-pack, not a six-pack. The attention his abs garner provides him with rewards like a sense of importance and a sense of significance. This motivates him to go to the gym and work on his body to maintain it. Why? Because it satisfies his strong need for personal importance. He loves it so much, he's turning it into a career and is already very successful at it. He has tapped into a natural talent that also satisfies a fundamental need.

There are many ways you can experience personal importance;

however, like all needs, they're not always positive or good for you. Having the best drugs in town, getting tattoos, being part of a gang, racing a car dangerously, owning the biggest house on the street, or knowing the history of a country might be what gets you going. Winning at your favorite board game or being the best at Scrabble because you studied the two-letter Scrabble words could make you feel smart and accomplished. Having clever or athletic kids or a beautiful spouse on your arm is one of hundreds of ways to feel good, and we all use the ones we feel work for us.

Check in with yourself to ensure you're using the best and most beneficial ways of increasing your sense of personal importance.

Ever notice you don't like to do things you're not good at? This is because they don't give you the feeling of being unique, important, or like you're making a difference. Ideally, you'll find positive ways to meet those needs rather than negative ones.

These are human needs, and you'll meet them no matter what. Positively. Negatively or neutrally. You'll find a way to feel significant.

What are your ways?

Passion

Human beings need passion, ranging from physical to sexual passion, to sports, and to the passion driving us to pursue our interests and professional endeavors.

When you understand your hot buttons and what vehicles will best serve your needs in a positive way, you'll be able to create a plan to meet those needs at the highest possible level.

If you cannot meet this need through a passionate hobby like playing football, or volleyball, or whatever you love, you might learn to do it through other vehicles like an argument, for instance. This will meet your need for passion even if you think it doesn't.

I've worked with many couples no longer enjoying passionate intimate times who have resorted to arguments and fights. Sometimes, this results in great make-up sex. Our need for passion is a big one, and we'll satisfy it however we can.

Perhaps, back in the cavemen days, our needs were met by almost dying every day trying to catch our meals. A messed-up drive-through order doesn't qualify by comparison. But being mission and purpose-driven toward what you were meant to do will almost always provide an outlet for this need and a rush of passion endorphins produced naturally.

Try removing all drugs, alcohol, food addictions, and distractions like video games, porn, gambling, complaining, and random shopping habits, and watch your energy rise, channeled toward your real purpose. You'll be pleasantly surprised. Amazed, even.

Learning and Growth

Most of us desire growth. If you're not growing your life, you're dying.

We like to feel as if we're moving forward personally and professionally. Since you're reading this book, chances are good that you like to stretch your wings too. Some people love school so much they never finish. They don't want to leave the school environment because, for them, there's a great deal of certainty and comfort in learning and education.

We need to grow. We need to learn.

Focus your studies on materials specifically chosen with your goals in mind, and you'll see immediate progress.

We are, without a doubt, more alive when we're learning something new, no matter what it is. From a new job, to games, to meeting a new loved one while learning about their interests.

Most people were taught that learning stops after formal education, and they go from learning to being entertained. The problem is that entertainment, as much as it meets our needs for variety, misses the mark when it comes to growth.

Think about when you first rode a bike, when mom or dad could finally let go of the back of the bike, and you did it! You experienced exhilaration! Why? You expanded who you were!

Visiting a new country, trying new food, or playing a new game makes us feel alive. Growth equals progress, and progress makes us happy.

If you want to be happier, make growing a habit for yourself.

You'll need to manage your mind's fear of new things and worry that this unknown experience might be harmful. Try to catch yourself when this happens. Maybe you're going to order a new dish at a restaurant, but you say, "I'll have what I know I always like." You know you'll have pleasure if you order what's familiar. It takes effort and risk to try another dish and risk it not being better.

Much of your life is lived this way. Your brain likes what it knows, and it's always campaigning to get you to stick with what you know. Sure, something new could be a six out of ten experience for you, but there's a chance the new experience will be a five, four, one, or minus digits. Your brain works hard to keep you from learning or trying new and different things.

"What if?" are common words used by this part of your brain. You'll have to learn to overcome the habit of staying with what you know. Challenge yourself to think of happiness as trying new things. If your brain says otherwise, ignore it if the new thing is not immoral or physically harmful. You'll feel safer plunging ahead, knowing your resistance is just fear speaking.

Try new, easy things at first. Drive home a different way. Try a new cuisine. Read a book by a new author. Go to a different place for the holidays. Join a mastermind group of powerhouse individuals who will push and stretch you. Check out M1, Gobundance, or the Epic Life Blueprint Community on Facebook.

Contribution

We all have a desire to do more than just live our lives, eat our meals, pay our bills, and go to the movies occasionally.

Life is about evolving. Most of us want to look back on our lives and see a steady progression. We want to know we've made an impact somehow. We want to know we've helped others through our efforts.

For me, life is about leaving a legacy, contributing to other's successes, and helping them overcome struggles. Helping people is extremely gratifying.

There are so many ways you can contribute to the world. You can volunteer for causes you believe in. You can contribute by giving your time or money or simply lending an ear. You can contribute by being the best you can be.

Our true purpose is not always something we find at an early age. It took a while to articulate mine; however, today it fulfills me to help others live full and happy lives. I give them the tools and success principles that allow them to meet their human needs at the highest level.

Most of us are happiest when we're connected. We want to feel we belong. Part of my contribution to others is helping them feel like a part of something. They're my tribe!

How do you fulfill your need to contribute in the world and make a difference?

We've covered a lot of ground. Take a minute to think about the hierarchy of needs.

Comfort Zone
Variety and Uncertainty
Community and Connection
Personal Importance
Passion
Learning and Growth
Contribution

Which need stands out to you? Rank them in order of importance to your overall sense of well-being and happiness. There's no right or wrong answer here, only what's true for you. Use your journal for this or mark them here.

———————————————————————————

———————————————————————————

———————————————————————————

———————————————————————————

———————————————————————————

These needs are the driving forces motivating everything you do. They can drive you to achieve great things, or they can motivate you to veer off your desired path into self-destructive behaviors. They can produce fear that will derail you. Or ideas that will change the world.

Look at your fears. Ask yourself where fear could be running your life or holding you back.

I watched my father work most of his life chained to his desk every weekend. He didn't play with me because he was addicted to working. Work became his identity. Work met his need to be in control, and since he was socially awkward, he went to work all the time to meet his need for certainty. Because of a bad financial decision, he had to work every weekend to catch up which allowed him to avoid the pain of socializing.

Who would demand that he socialize when he had bills to pay? He found a way to stay safe and stay stuck. See how clever our minds are at keeping us safe but not happy? It's a trap. Don't get stuck there.

I watched my dad do this his whole life. His debt was so high when he died, I had to cash in my retirement savings to assist with his funeral arrangements. My father worked very hard, but had nothing to show for it at the end of his life.

I decided I'd never be in debt or without money. I feared being without money so much I worked very hard and became much more frugal with my money. I managed my money more consciously because of the pain I witnessed and experienced. I started working out a lot, going to the gym for comfort, significance, personal importance, variety, and connection to others.

Aristotle said, "We are what we repeatedly do."

Tony Robbins says, "If you meet three of your needs at a high level, they become addictions."

Look at what you're doing, look at the way your needs are being met, and determine if they support the epic life you're building or if they'll lead you to becoming enslaved like my father.

I've taken up yoga and meditation to balance out my overworked muscle of working hard. I've had to let go of gambling and drugs I once used to quiet and relax my mind from overworking and not being able to still my thoughts. I always tried to do more and be more until it took its toll, and I had to back up, and find a better way.

What are your needs that might be off balance and in need of some attention?

Some people are amazing fathers or mothers and never workout. Or they're in debt because they fear working and being rejected. Some people allow the overall fear of not being good enough to stop them from success and acting. They use being a "good parent" or "spiritual person" to hide their real fears. Do you know anyone like this? Perhaps intimately?

Awareness is the first step to change. And we're building new habits before the chains become too strong to break.

Your fears will determine your behavior and action (or lack of action), so let's look at these. As always, write them in your journal or in the space provided.

Action Steps

- **Use your journal to list your top three fears, or write them here.**

_____

_____

Fear determines your focus. Look at yours to see if you notice a pattern or theme. What causes the most suffering in your life today? Here is an opportunity to evolve and grow. Suffering is a choice or a lack of awareness.

Most people don't realize their fears can serve them if they find the gift hidden within them. Your fear can be a great motivator to never experience loneliness, or being poor, or being last to be picked for a team.

The first step is to identify your fears. Then you can come up with a strategy to overcome them.

- **List a way to overcome each of the fears you identified above.**

_____

_____

_____

_____

What will motivate you to get out of bed in the morning? What will cause you to stay late at the office, to put in more effort where you need it most? Right now, your fear may be causing you to avoid certain things. Spend some time working out a way to use your fears to your advantage.

To direct your strongest desires in focused ways, despite any discomfort you might feel, you must keep your motivators in mind as you work through your hot buttons and tap into unbelievable motivation, passion, and drive. When you understand why you do what you do and why you don't do what you know you should be doing, you can motivate and inspire yourself to take action, and get the results you're seeking.

To assist you, I created an acronym: HISTEP.

H=Headliner

Are there any emotional states you'd do almost anything to avoid? As an example, most people would do anything to avoid humiliation or embarrassment, one of the primary reasons people don't like public speaking. Instead of trying to avoid these emotions or letting them stop you, I'm going to teach you how to use them to propel you forward.

Most of us also want, and even crave, a certain degree of personal significance or attention. In my seminars, I teach a simple strategy for achieving this—act in private the same way you'd behave in public.

If you master this, when you get on the main stage of your life, you don't have to modify your behavior; you just step up and keep doing what you were doing behind closed doors.

When you behave one way behind closed doors and another way in public, you experience stress. Your integrity muscle hasn't been developed, and you risk reverting to your private behavior, especially when under stress. For this reason, professional athletes practice and play with the same rituals.

When in doubt, ask yourself if the benefits of whatever you want to do outweigh the embarrassment and humiliation you'd experience if your actions were exposed on the front page of tomorrow's newspaper or on social media. Make sure your headlines are ones you can live with. Use this fear of embarrassment and humiliation to your benefit. Your brain is either tricking you or you're tricking it. Pick wisely.

I=Imagination

Albert Einstein said your imagination is the preview of coming attractions.

How is your trailer? Is it a comedy? Romance? Success story? Or is it a horror story? What are you pre-playing in your imagination and manifesting in your future?

A famous study was done on basketball players, broken into three groups. The first group practiced every day, five hours each day, working on drills and actual on-court practice. The second group spent their time visualizing their game, imagining themselves hitting their shots, and doing the physical movements perfectly without the basketball. The third group never moved their bodies. They focused their minds on events happening as they wished they would. They literally never touched a basketball, except in their minds.

Several months later, after careful monitoring, it was discovered that the players wound up with virtually the same results and success.

This drives home an incredibly powerful point about your power to create your results. All things created in our world are created twice. The first time in our minds and the second time physically. All forms of creation and invention started as a picture in the creator's mind before they became a physical thing. Imagining things can be just as powerful as experiencing them.

Jack Nicholas is famous for saying he would not hit a golf shot until he had pre-played in his mind the entire shot up to the ball landing and rolling into the hole. He's considered one of the greatest golfers of all time, clocked during his famous Masters victory with the same pre-shot routine—within one second for every shot.

When Greg Norman had his infamous Masters meltdown, he had a six-stroke lead heading into the final nine holes but was clocked speeding up with virtually each shot.

When I was cold-calling three days a week as a real-estate agent, I used to imagine people searching for the number of a real-estate broker saying, "Honey, we need to find the name of a realtor, so we can sell our house." I would imagine their joy when I called them. I would feel the feelings, see a clear picture of the scene unfolding on the other end of the phone, and I would be motivated to make more calls. I expected to get a good response and; therefore, I was better positioned to receive one.

What you expect you often get. The key is not to live in fear of "not getting it" but to remain positively open and optimistic.

Start focusing on what you want to create and on the feelings your successes will generate as though they're already happening. The positive results you're seeking will start showing up more and more.

Revisit the lists you created earlier of your results and desired outcomes. Picture the entire process in your mind. Imagine how you will feel. Imagine it being even better than you imagine. Of all methods to self-motivate, setting goals and focusing on them often may be the most under used by amateurs. Yet, it's the most powerful among professionals. Something to think about.

S=Scarcity

Scarcity is a concept used by marketers to create a sense of urgency or demand based upon a limited supply. It works because "having enough" is a core element of survival for all animals, especially humans.

Retailers learned this when trying to find a way to increase traditionally slow, after-Christmas sales. They discovered that by limiting the supply of the season's most popular toys, they could create a scarcity factor in the marketplace, ensuring a hefty profit, and high demand during the holidays and long after, well into the previously slow months of January and February.

So, how can this scarcity thing work to your advantage?

Apply the "what if" game to everything you do. For example, what if this is the last time you get to play soccer? What if this is your last kiss? What if this is your last meal, the last time you get to lie in the sun, or deliver a presentation? When you make a habit of thinking like this, you'll more readily focus your energy and not pass up opportunities.

"Either you're tricking your mind, or it's tricking you."
RockThomas

You'll find yourself appreciating what you already have and grateful for your opportunities. Your attitude of gratitude will infuse your body, and you'll start to show up in life with more passion and more energy. You'll start giving off a vibe people will be attracted to.

Think of the last day on a vacation, how you start to say things like, "This is the last day on the beach," or "This is the last meal overlooking the lake," or, "This is the last game of golf." Think about how the experience itself seems to have a different value to it.

What about the last day of work before a holiday? How focused are you? How effective? Because your brain has made things important and urgent, you probably did three times more work than usual.

T=Triple E (EEE)

Extreme emotional experiences can be positive or negative. You never forget these experiences. They're so profound, and they affect your neurology in such a deep way, they become a permanent part of your being. We may not remember the details of what was said or how things unfolded, but we always remember how these events made us feel. A ticket you got while speeding or a broken-bone experience. Where you were when a celebrity you admired died or abuse you experienced at the hands of a boss. The firing of a loved one. A romantic moment that touched your soul or a near-miss car accident.

I recently visited a temple in Vietnam with children who suffer from water on the brain at birth, causing their brains to grow three times the size of others, causing incredible pain. They can only lie unmoving and crying most of the time. Meeting them created such an impact on me that I cancelled all my shopping plans and took the money I'd earmarked for buying souvenirs and personal items and donated it to the temple. I cried, felt deeply sad, and grateful, all at the same time. I did something for children in need and gained a new appreciation for my health. This is a EEE.

You may have a burning desire to re-create an emotional experience because it was exhilarating, or you might never want to experience it again because of the deep pain it caused you. Maybe you caught the winning touchdown for your high school football team. Maybe you gave your school's graduation speech or won an award for being the most consistent, dedicated student.

Oprah, Terry Fox, Michael Jordan, and Mark Zuckerberg all had a negative triple E and it's something they never want to experience again. Maybe you have too. In their cases, they took the pain of disappointment and turned it into fuel for achievement. Not forgetting pain, but using it as leverage, is what passionate successful people do.

Vince Lombardi said, "Show me a good loser, and I'll show you a loser".

I interpret that to mean that a winner hates to lose so much they don't let feelings of disappointment go unspent. They learn from each loss, and keep pushing.

Your job is to not smother emotions with food, booze, or drugs, but to harness them and use them as drive. To not be owned by the pain of your bad experiences but to use it as a catalyst.

We've all experienced some negatives or pain in our lives. You may have broken a bone, went through a divorce, had a sick child, or lost a parent. These extreme emotional events shape our lives because of the meaning we attach to them.

After Oprah was raped, she decided to take that event and draw power from it, to transform herself. She used her EEE to help other people by sharing what she learned on her way to healing. Through the authenticity of her pain, she empowered others.

When Michael Jordan didn't make his high-school varsity basketball team, he used the experience and figuratively stuck a knife in himself, over and over, as he reviewed the pain caused by failure until he really felt it. The burst of renewed pain drove home how much he never wanted to feel that pain again. He went on to practice harder than he had before, harder than anyone else, and the rest is history.

What most people do is the exact opposite; they numb the pain, with food or drugs, or some other addiction, losing the very drive pain provides for those brave enough to endure it, and work through it.

Terry Fox, cancer activist and marathon runner, walked almost all the way across Canada on one leg.

Mark Zuckerberg founded Facebook because he was rejected by a fraternity, and his heart was broken by a girl. He created his own place to belong, and he never looked back.

What pain can you use as a springboard to better things? What pain do you numb, robbing yourself of the fuel you need to take your life to the next level?

Once, a business partner defaulted on their 2.6-million-dollar commitment to me. The pain fueled me to start several more businesses and recoup this money within eighteen months. Through those businesses, I found my life purpose and many of my best friends in my mastermind organization M1.

You never know which adversity will uncover your life's mission if you're open to staying in the pain and getting the lesson out of it. For me, this skill came later in life. Hopefully, for you, it might happen earlier if you're open to it sooner.

A few years ago, I tore my triceps muscle off my elbow experiencing perhaps the most pain ever in my life; however, this led me to learning how to workout in far less time than what I had been doing (ninety minutes per day). Now, I'm able to get a brilliant workout in less than fifteen minutes.

To rehab, and sustain my progress with restricted use, I had to become educated. Which, because I was open, and followed Rule #9—become a meaning master—I learned a better method than the old model I was following.

Sometimes, being broken down gives us a chance to look at things with a fresh perspective.

When Japan was bombed in WW2, many of their factories were demolished, and upon having to start from scratch, they realized they could build a whole new model that was more effective than the Band-Aid modifications they were used to making on existing factories.

One can harness the energy in emotionally charged events to create greatness in your life or let it destroy you. Each EEE carries with it a seed of possibility. Successful people seek it, find it, and use it. And now you can too.

The concept of fight or flight is one we're all familiar with, and most of us have experienced both responses at some points in our lives. Still, we usually favor one over the other as a typical reaction to emotional events.

My father was very demanding and expected a lot from his children around our farm. I fed twenty-two horses before breakfast and, being the youngest of six children, ate leftovers and took cold baths. I dug holes, fixed fences in the winter with holes in my gloves, and if I came crying into the house with frozen fingers and toes, my father would send me back out, telling me, "Don't come back until the job is done."

Later in life, stranded in Asia after losing my traveler's checks, I called him, asking him to wire me money.

"Son, you got yourself there, you can get yourself home," he said.

For part of my life, I longed for a father who was proud of me and loved me, and I resented him for the pain he caused me by not providing those emotions.

It took a long time for me to realize my father, who had been abandoned as a child, had done the best he could with what he learned. Inadvertently, he'd raised me to be tenacious, resourceful, and hard working. That was the benefit of the programing he downloaded to me.

I'm grateful for the resources he gave me. They rarely felt good in the moment; however, they carried raw fuel of massive exponential ability that rocketed me forward.

If you feel like you're getting kicked by life then you're most likely playing the victim, and every time you do that you spend your valuable "adversity energy" which is an asset to be used for personal transformation, not on blaming life, people, or circumstances. Either way, you have this energy that has been manufactured within you for your transformation or for your deterioration. Like so many things that make up your life, it's your choice.

What events in your life have left you feeling resentful? Think about experiences you have had without your consent or events that were uncomfortable, but caused you to grow. Without going into moral, ethical, or legal aspects and judgments, you have an opportunity to view these experiences from a different perspective. You can become the victor and become stronger, using the energy to move you forward. You only have to decide to do so.

Whenever I'm faced with an emotionally charged event, I always ask myself, "What's great about this?" and, "What can I learn from this?"

Asking these questions will help you tap into the power of your triple Es. If you try to mute them, ignore them, or begin to play the "poor me" card, you'll rob yourself of the fruit, the life-giving nectar these events are bringing you.

We'll talk more about re-framing in chapter nine.

E=Exaggeration

I'm not smarter or more creative than anyone else. But, I can create a sense of urgency for myself in much of what I do. Perhaps it's in my genes, or maybe I picked it up building fences in thirty-below-zero-degree weather as a kid. I like to think it's because urgency has become a habit, a habit I continue because it works.

Successful people schedule tasks into their lives. They handle events and demands before they become important and urgent. They avoid waiting until the last possible moment, operating in crisis mode, and acting at the last minute. This behavior doesn't allow for proper pacing and forces unneeded stress into one's life.

We all know people who subconsciously thrive on this type of uncertainty, seeming to enjoy the bit of personal importance they feel having to rush about handling insignificant events that have now become significant due to poor planning. They must E-mail that document urgently, and you're stopping them. Or they must rush across town to do their taxes on the last day, and it's not their fault they will miss the company party or be fashionably late. They cannot come to the picnic with you because they must take care of that assignment or they must renew their passport. Do you know people like this? Are you one of them?

The DNA of the epic life blueprint includes the development of a sense of urgency and exaggerates it, so we schedule, and get things done in advance, reduce unnecessary stress, and we're able to focus on the task at hand.

Scheduling is such a powerful, simple tool. If you use it, your level of stress will drop by 80%. You'll live longer, and you'll live better, because you won't react to things like the average person. You'll be back in the driver's seat.

Stephan Covey has a great piece on this regarding the four quadrants of time management. Read it in his classic book *The Seven Habits of Highly Effective People*.

Action Step

- **Use your journal or this book to list two things you've been putting off that you'll schedule today and why doing these things is important to you (remember, when you exaggerate the consequences, you either trick your brain or it will trick you).**

_____

_____

_____

_____

_____

_____

_____

_____

_____

_____

_____

_____

_____

_____

_____

_____

_____

_____

_____

_____

_____

P=People

A few years ago, I was determined to upgrade my peer group to a whole new level, so I went on a search for a mastermind group to join. I was surprised to discover most groups were nothing more than a glad-handing, coffee drinking, business networking group of people who didn't inspire me.

So, I created my own group. Three years later, I'm compelled to be a better person around these likeminded individuals, and I'm proud to say I've influenced them too.

Could your group use an upgrade? If you don't have a group, check out Gobundance, M1, or the Epic Life Blueprint Community on Facebook.

Most of us have a strong emotional need for connection, community, and belonging. We want to be part of something and fit in with our peers. We want to please people. We want to feel as if we belong, at work, at home, and with our family and friends. Your peer group has power over you, whether you like it or not.

Seek out a peer group that's going to support you and encourage you to succeed. Find people who you aspire to be like or who do what you long to do. It's not necessary to reinvent the wheel. There are successful role models for just about anything out there.

Look at the people you typically hang out with, and ask yourself how they rub off on you. Are they negative or positive? Are they healthy or unhealthy? Do they have good habits or bad habits?

Think about the way you talk to yourself. Are you your best friend? Most people are their own toughest critic. We may be the first to compliment and acknowledge other people, but don't acknowledge our own worth often enough.

Surrounding yourself with people who make you feel good, and are walking the path you wish to travel, will propel you toward your goals.

Being accountable to another individual is a powerful motivator to stick to your schedule and commitments. We generally won't blow-off a meeting when there are others depending on us. Community and sharing bring out the best in us, so be sure to put yourself into an environment that brings out the best in you.

I joke with my audiences and tell them I hang around with people who are smarter, wealthier, more creative, and happier than I'm, and when they don't want to hang around with me anymore, I pay them to spend time with me. I hire them as my coaches. You'll end up speaking, eating, acting, behaving, and getting similar results as those you spend time with, so set yourself up to win by choosing winners.

Over the past few years, I've spent time with the Tony Robbins Platinum Partnership, T. Harv Eker, A-Fest, Gobundance, M1, YPO, Re/Max, and Keller Williams. Fortunately, anyone can learn from these outstanding resources as most have websites full of helpful information.

Action Step

- **Write down these six hot buttons and carry them with you, post them on your fridge, bathroom mirror, or in your car (somewhere you can see them and review them regularly).**

H=Headliner
I=Imagination
S=Scarcity
T=Triple E
E=Exaggeration
P=People

When you're feeling down or going through a stressful or emotional time, check your hot buttons and determine which are being activated.

Ask yourself, "What's great about this? How can I use these feelings to move me toward my goals instead of pushing me away from them?"

At the same time, ask yourself which of your needs or emotions are threatened and which you want to move toward the most.

Comfort Zone
Variety and Uncertainty

Community and Connection
Personal Importance
Passion
Learning and Growth
Contribution

Learn to make the most of every situation by taking control, with clear understanding and purpose, and the support of those around you. Own up to your feelings and hot buttons, maximizing the ones that work for you and minimizing those that don't.

Three Things to Act on

Before completing the next step, look in a mirror and say: "I understand success comes from the implementation of knowledge, not the acquisition of it; therefore, I choose to step into an epic life by taking action on my new-found knowledge. As I read, I will capture the ideas that resonate with me and apply them to my life until I master them. Period. This is what badasses do, and I'm a badass. The result of these committed actions is an epic life!"

Action Step

- **Based on what you learned in this chapter, record three things in your journal or below that you're committed to acting on. Take as much space as you need to outline not only what you'll act upon, but how (steps you'll take), and the all-important why (your reason and result motivations and expectations). Write:**

I commit to take action on:

_____
_____
_____
_____
_____
_____
_____
_____

I commit to take action on:

_____
_____
_____
_____
_____
_____
_____
_____

I commit to take action on:

_____
_____

_____

_____

_____

_____

_____

_____

CHAPTER FOUR RECAP

➢ The hierarchy of needs outlines the fundamental emotional requirements all humans need to survive and to thrive, from the most basic to the more advanced. Discover your most prevalent needs, and learn what vehicles you use to meet them.

> ComfortZone
> Variety and Uncertainty
> Community and Connection
> Personal Importance
> Passion
> Learning and Growth
> Contribution

➢ Fear determines your focus. Look at yours to see if you notice a pattern or theme.

➢ Be conscious of your hot buttons and review them regularly. Self-motivation is heightened with self-awareness.

> **H**=Headliner
> **I**=Imagination
> **S**=Scarcity
> **T**=Triple E
> **E**=Exaggeration
> **P**=People

CHAPTER FIVE PREVIEW

*Sharpen your focus, decrease your distractions,
and increase your results.*

"Begin with the end in mind"
Stephan Covey

Chapter Five

"For every disciplined action, there are multiple rewards."
Jim Rohn

A successful person is an average person, focused.

Winston Churchill said, "Uninterrupted, continuous effort is more powerful than strength and intelligence."

Have you ever noticed highly successful people seem obsessed with what they are doing 24/7?

A great movie illustrating how a highly successful person can be consumed by something he is passionate about is *Social Networking*, the story of Mark Zuckerberg, creator of Facebook. He was a guy totally consumed by his passion. Nothing took him off his path, and he became the leader of one of the most successful companies in the world and a very rich man.

Most of us have a hard time staying that focused. We get distracted by our cell phones, social media, and the burning need to check this or check that. You may find you're rarely in the zone where you have a continuous stream of focused energy.

Studies have shown that multitasking reduces creativity and increases stress. Stop giving yourself the luxury of being distracted by small conversations or social pop-ups and anything you allow to ding you into distraction.

Schedule your success and follow through. Be like a magnifying glass, focusing the Sun's energy on one spot and igniting it into flames, or the airplane that goes full throttle for about a minute before attaining lift off. When you focus your greatest energy up front like this, you ultimately get to cruise and enjoy the ride much more.

"If it's not scheduled, it doesn't exist."
Rock Thomas

Even Mark Zuckerberg focused his energy for several years before his breakthrough. There's no magic pill. No one is going to hand you success on a silver platter. You're going to have to make some sacrifices along the way and put some aspects of your life on the back burner. There's no such thing as time management. There is only prioritizing and execution.

When I was running my real-estate businesses, I outworked my competition every day and felt confident a heavy workload would never knock me out of the race. This focus, this work ethic, was developed during my childhood, growing up on the farm and working odd jobs.

What if you don't have this work ethic ingrained in you? You'll need to develop your work ethic, and make it your habit. Solid work habits are common in all successful people.

During my days as a McDonalds employee, my manager came to me and said, "John is sick, and I need you to do the best job you can cleaning the lobby area on your own today."

Normally, two of us cleaned the lobby. Now, I would be alone. This was my chance to shine, to stand out, to have my need for personal importance met, and be recognized for my ability. Unknowingly, my manager had pushed one of my hot buttons and motivated me to double my efforts. I utilized this focused energy to be more effective. The lobby looked fantastic, and I received a promotion. Was it because I was more intelligent than my co-workers? No. Was it because I was more consistent and more focused with my energy? Yes. Was I dedicated to my personal work ethic? Yes! I was willing to do whatever it took to achieve success, and my determination made all the difference. Knowing doing a good job would give me the feelings of "personal importance" (one of the basic human needs), I let it motivate me into action.

I took flying lessons at the age of fifteen. My instructor, seeing how diligent and committed I was, offered to pay for 90% of the airplane and invited me to buy the other 10% so we could purchase an aircraft together. If I could go the extra mile, it would create opportunities. But, to make this happen, I needed to raise a lot of money in a short period. I was motivated!

This time, the opportunity to meet my needs (in this case, community) popped up. I decided to harvest tobacco to raise the money I needed. I went down to southern Ontario and learned how to pick tobacco, working long, brutal hours for six weeks. I never gave up, although 80% of the people who started the job with me ended up quitting. Without a clear reason or need being fulfilled, this intense job would take most people out in a very short period.

Almost any job, project, task, or goal will eventually take people out who lack clarity of reason, or a defining need, so I urge you to get clear about the reasons behind your goals and for everything you do. This focus will result in massive power.

If I RRAFTed this goal, my result would be to become a pilot. The reasons were because I wanted to be recognized and admired. Additionally, I wanted to make my dad proud. Not only did I have one reason, I had several, which is essential to achieving big goals.

If you want to be motivated to take uncommon amounts of action, and to be truly inspired, then you must not just have a physical goal (in my case, buying a plane or becoming a pilot). Your success will come down to the emotional component of the goal that provides the fire and the fuel needed to propel you forward. At age fifteen, owning an airplane was a big goal!

Finding your reasons, and being clear about them, is critical if you're going to succeed at attaining any goal you set for yourself.

To achieve my goal, the action I took was to find the most economical way of paying for my lessons. I found a short-term, well-paying job and stuck with it. Focusing on how I would feel once I become a pilot, and on the pride of owning a plane, kept me taking uncommon action to complete a grueling job picking tobacco when many others quit. It was not that I was stronger physically than the others; my goals were more compelling and more emotionalized. In the end, I experienced the thrill of being one of the few who made it to the finish line. When the job ended, I spent three days in bed, tired, sick, and worn out. It didn't matter though, because I had achieved my goal of raising the money to buy into a plane. My body knew where the finish line was. My mind, my work ethic, and my focused energy brought me there.

I'm confident you can do the same thing. The will to succeed is a muscle you can develop, providing you tap into the end emotional result you're after.

Rereading chapter four several times will help you master this ability.

Deciding what you want is easier said than done. Why? Most people don't know what they want. We've talked about how our brains are wired to help us avoid pain and how this automatic thinking leads us to focus on what we don't want. Accept this as human wiring, and know you can rewire yourself.

When you build your RRAFT, using focused energy, take the time to decide what you want and commit to that, no matter what. If things you don't want pop up, either reframe the thought or push it away for now.

When you do this, I promise your results will increase. If you're a sales professional, I encourage you to start prospecting early in the day or early in the evening, once the phone has stopped ringing and emails taper off. Be available when everyone else has gone home. Focus on your goals and their personal meaning for you, always.

I used to set an appointment and schedule time for prospecting between 6:30 and 8:30 in the evenings, on Mondays, Tuesdays, and Wednesdays. I'd go into my office and close the door. I accepted no phone calls and turned off my email. I strictly focused on building new business during this time. And it worked.

Successful people treat prospecting like an appointment. This is one of the main differences between average sales people and ones who hit their goals consistently.

I knocked on more doors than anybody in my office. I made more calls than anybody in my office. I listened to more audio programs than anybody in my office, and I took more courses than anybody in my office. As a result, the owner of the agency offered to sell me the company. Why? Once again, my work ethic drew opportunity to me. My focused energy paid off.

Try it. I think you'll like the results you see. One caveat—you need to be patient, for it may take some time to see your breakthrough. Everything you're doing to build your epic life blueprint; however, will help you get there faster. Each piece speeds the process and adds to your new solid foundation.

What are you doing that's going to move you ahead of your competition? What are you doing today that's better than yesterday? How are you out-working others and out-learning them (and yourself)? How are you more focused and more disciplined?

Maximize your efforts, and promote your abilities.

Action Step

- **List three ways you can outwork your competition. Here are some ideas:**

  Show up early.
  Stay late.
  Offer to help in another department.
  Shadow someone you want to learn from.
  Ask a leader or mentor to lunch.
  Work for free (for education purposes).
  Say yes without knowing to what.

_____

_____

It's much easier to be motivated when you know what your hot buttons are and when you press them daily. The "law of repetition" will be on your side. Knowing your motivational hot buttons also helps you recognize environments and opportunities where you know others will consciously or unconsciously press them for you.

I was playing at a golf tournament recently, and somebody came up to me and said, "Oh yeah, well you're a motivational speaker, Rock. But let's see what you can do today."

They pressed a button that challenged me by testing my reputation and my identity.

One of the strongest forces in human nature is the desire and need to stay congruent with how we describe ourselves. Knowing that, you can go out and tell people who you are at your best, and watch your unconscious triggers strive to live up to it as I did that day.

I focused my energy and gained leverage to play well. I ended up with a hole in one, shooting the second lowest score of the day in a competitive event. How's that for using my hot-button's energy in a positive way?

Focused energy is about staying present and making what you're doing the most important thing at that time. Pay attention to your hot buttons in relation to your energy level, and watch your results soar to higher and higher levels.

Remember, clarity leads to power. Knowing what you value, care about, and want, allows you to stay focused.

Action Step

- **Use your journal to list three things (hot buttons) that really get you fired up, or record them here.**

_____

_____

_____

_____

Integrate these ideas into your life by doing more than anyone ever expected. Activate the "law of going the extra mile". For example, I used to pretend as though somebody was watching my work, and I did my very best every time.

When you do things like this, you build new neural pathways in your brain utilizing focused energy. Ultimately, if you keep it up, these new routes become main roads in your mind. You create new neuro associations—literally rewiring yourself to perform better.

Your ability to stay focused will separate you from the masses of average people. Most people make the mistake of looking for an easier way to do things in any situation. This is known as the "size of the problem law". Your mind tends to freak out if a problem seems too big. Don't do this.

People who are interested in success don't achieve success or find success. People who are committed to success, achieve success. They don't let anything stand in the way, period. One of the best ways to combat the human urge to take the easy way out is to break whatever you wish to achieve down into manageable, bite-sized tasks. Once you've set your big goal, as contrary as this may seem, concentrate only on the small tasks at hand (not on the big picture) until you near the end, having completed most of the steps required to achieve your goal. Now the size problem will seem manageable.

> _"If you refuse to accept anything but the_
> _very best, you'll very often get it."_
> W. Somerset Maugham

Over the next few days, pay attention to how many times you get distracted. How often do you seek a less painful solution than the one you know you should be doing? When things get tough, what do you fall back on? What vices do you activate to take away the pain or the sting of not achieving what you want? What do you use to avoid the work you know you need to do to get where you want to go?

Many people before you have faced trials and tribulations on their path to success and have run squarely into the wall of frustration. You're not alone, and all the decisions you've made prior to this have brought you to where you are. Now, it's time to take responsibility for the rest of your life, and learn from your experiences, so you can develop more effective and focused energy.

When you catch yourself saying, "I have to do this," change your words to, "I choose to do this." Develop a pattern of positive language surrounding your choices.

I choose to take my kids to hockey.
I choose to go to the party tonight.
I choose to work late tonight.
I choose to pay my taxes today.
I choose to pay my bills.
I choose not to pay my bills.

As you use this pattern of language, you'll become more empowered. As you take more responsibility for your life, you'll start to make better choices by default. By saying "I choose", you'll own your actions and be motivated to make better ones.

I choose to learn. I choose to read this book and improve my life by understanding the principles of success. I choose, I choose, I choose.

When you do the easy things in life, life will be difficult. When you do what's challenging, or difficult, life will be easy. Get the hard stuff out of the way up front.

Brian Tracy says, "Eat the frog first!" which means take care of unpleasant tasks or difficult work first thing. Then, the rest of your day or project will be easy and more enjoyable.

Studies are clear that our energy levels are highest in the mornings and; therefore, waiting to workout at the end of the day or handling demanding meetings or calls in the middle of the afternoon is strategically wrong. Every choice counts. Learn to work smarter, not harder.

Does success take a lot of energy? It does. Does failure take a lot of energy? Absolutely! If you're just working to pay the bills, that takes energy! If you're going to spend a lot of energy on anything, then spend everything you have in the direction of what you want.

Action Step

- **Using your journal (or the space below), take thirty seconds and write what you want (no editing). Avoid writing what you don't want. Remember the "law of how you do anything is how you do everything". Don't skip steps.**

_____

_____

_____

_____

_____

_____

_____

_____

I was out to dinner the other night with some friends who have an energetic seven-year-old daughter. And, bless the parents, they don't try to mute her energy. It occurred to me that most of us have held back from expressing ourselves fully at one point or another because of something someone else said or impressed upon us.

What energy have you muted in yourself? How many times have you held back from expressing yourself or from going for it out of hesitation or fear that something bad or embarrassing might happen?

Don't hold it back. Let it out! Release it! Let it fly, and see what happens. Your boundaries are only your current limits, and they can be expanded indefinitely.

Water runs faster when the walls of a river are narrow, and it slows down when the river opens into a lake. If you focus your energy like the walls of the Grand Canyon, making it very narrow and very tall, there's only one place for the river of your energy to flow—straight toward your target. You'll be a force to be reckoned with.

Muhammad Ali practiced in the mornings and, though he didn't love every practice, he loved everything that came from his strong work ethic. He said, "I hated every minute of training, but I said, 'Don't quit. Suffer now, and live the rest of your life as a champion!'"

You may not love every practice either, or rehearsing every script, or preparing for every meeting. When you pay your dues up front, success begins to take on its own momentum. An object in motion remains in motion. When you're confident you can outwork anyone, nobody will be able to compete with you.

Law of Discipline: Pay the Price of Practice in Private to Perform Epically in Public.

I encourage you to say "yes" before your brain can say "no" because your brain is going to try to talk you out of anything outside your comfort zone.

Ask yourself why when you want to say no. Talk yourself into saying yes until it becomes a habit. What we say to ourselves matters the most. The power of why allows you to associate positive emotions with positive results. These emotions give you staying power.

Once you're clear on this, the how part will show up almost magically. Stop letting your worry over how or when you'll do something get in the way of following your heart and doing what you know needs to be done. Instead, find a way to make it work.

Action Steps

- **Use your journal (or the space below) to complete this exercise and answer the last question.**

  Write about an issue that's currently troubling you, why it's important for you to take action in this situation, and what action you're going to take.

  When you do this, what positive result will you enjoy?

_____

_____

_____

_____

_____

_____

_____

_____

_____

_____

_____

_____

_____

_____

_____

- **Take time this weekend to prepare for the upcoming week. Sunday is a good day to do this.**

During the process, review what you've written about so far. Review goals, and review the progress you've made. Use a simple spreadsheet to track your daily results (or whatever tool you've adopted to do this) and look over your previous week, month, and quarter. When you see improvement in things like fitness or training efforts, or business related matters like number of contacts in relation to sales made, that's exciting!

Recording and reviewing results are simple steps that achieve great results with hardly any effort. Your brain will like that part, though it may still resist the idea of doing something new. Convince it by giving it more emotional reasons why you'll follow through. Convince it by concentrating on the small step this exercise really is. Surely, you can spare a few minutes each day to jot down your results and a few more on Sunday to celebrate and learn from your progress?

As you review your goals, think again about why you want to reach them. I can't emphasize this enough. Picture what it will be like when you achieve your goal and how it will feel.

Three Things to Act on

Before completing the next step, look in a mirror and say: "I understand success comes from the implementation of knowledge, not the acquisition of it; therefore, I choose to step into an epic life by taking action on my new-found knowledge. As I read, I will capture the ideas that resonate with me and apply them to my life until I master them. Period. This is what badasses do, and I'm a badass. The result of these committed actions is an epic life!"

Action Step

- **Based on what you learned in this chapter, record three things in your journal or below that you're committed to acting on. Take as much space as you need to outline not only what you'll act upon, but how (steps you'll take), and the all-important why (your reason and result motivations and expectations). Write:**

I commit to take action on:

_____

_____

_____

_____

_____

_____

_____

_____

I commit to take action on:

_____

_____

_____

_____

_____

_____

_____

I commit to take action on:

_____

_____

_____

_____

_____

_____

_____

_____

Chapter Five Recap

➤ Your energy is highest in the morning. Do your most difficult tasks first. "Eat the frog".

➤ Develop an epic work ethic. Build new neuro-associations that will turn you into a badass!

➤ Pay attention to your hot buttons and triggers. Knowing what fires you up is extremely useful when motivating yourself. Knowing when and how to encourage others to fire off your buttons can be very motivating too.

➤ Take an hour on the weekend to plan your upcoming week. During this time, review your goals and your recent efforts to accomplish them. CSI yourself.

➤ That which is measured will improve. That which is measured and reported upon improves exponentially. Keep track of your efforts and stats. Don't skip this important step. Tracking motivates you as you see improvements, no matter how small.

CHAPTER SIX PREVIEW

*Some of your beliefs support you, and some don't.
Develop a mental blueprint to success, and toss
out old plans no longer serving you.*

CHAPTER SIX

Rule Six: Nurture your beliefs.

"What you tell yourself, you tend to experience."
Rock Thomas

I can do anything if I'm committed and creative.
Say yes, and figure it out later.
Everything happens for a reason, and that reason is here to
serve me.
There is no winning and losing, only winning
and learning.
Do what you fear, and it will disappear.

These are a few of the beliefs I nurture. They feed my life. I say nurture because to nurture is to support and encourage during a period of training and development. We're always developing as we go through life. It makes sense to support your efforts, and develop beliefs that will move you ahead rather than hold you back.

We all have a variety of beliefs. Some support us, and some don't. The ones that don't support us are often unconscious. They might manifest themselves as thoughts that go something like this:

"I'm not good enough or worthy of xyz."
"What if I fail?"
"I'm a procrastinator!"
"There's nothing I can do to change my situation or who I am."

"Some people are born with a natural ability to communicate, lead, or be funny."
"I don't have enough time, money, good looks, friends, energy, or fill in the blank."
"I'm different. I just don't fit in."

Beliefs are shortcuts to decisions. Their goal is to help us figure out what to do (or what not to do). Beliefs often work hand in hand with ego, which only wants to make you right. So, if we want to believe something enough, our egos will find evidence to support our disempowering beliefs, just to prove we're right and make our ego happy.

When you attach a meaning to something in your life, it's going to bring you pain or pleasure. If you believe you don't have enough time to read this entire book, then adding it to your schedule will translate into angst or pain, and you'll find ways to support your feelings. Soon, you won't find the time to finish this book.

However, if you decide to perceive reading this book as potential power for you to move forward and be more effective and efficient in your life, you'll see it as beneficial, and you'll find time. Because you believe it's important, you'll take action, and create the result in the real world that matches your internal picture, your belief.

Believing is creation. That's worth repeating. Believing is creation. You're either creating possibility or creating mental obstacles.

Saying "I can't" is a mental obstacle that's self-created. Saying "I'll try" is an upgrade. Saying "I'll do it" is an empowering belief. See the difference? None are true or false statements. They're merely your mind creating your reality.

Let's say you go to a wedding, and you believe you're not a good dancer. You tell people, "I'm not a dancer". You tried it before, and someone called you "two left feet" after you stepped on her feet twice. You spent your time apologizing, feeling like a klutz. You thought "I never want to do that again." You wrote in your mental operation's manual that dancing equals pain and that the best "belief" to use, which leads to decision making, is "I'm not a dancer". Whew! Your mind has kept you safe from pain. Its job is done. It has added something to your identity to keep you safe. Next time a dancing opportunity comes up, the decision is easy. It's "I'm not a dancer" or "I don't dance."

But one day, you have a few drinks, and you override the belief. You go out and have a blast. Nobody judges you, and you feel great. You connect with a lovely girl who tells you that you're a good dancer with great rhythm.

Your brain wants you to have pleasure, but its first job is protection. So, you form a new belief, an evolved one. "If I drink, I loosen up, and I'm a good dancer." Given a chance to dance, you might respond, "Sure, just let me have a few drinks to loosen up first."

To change your beliefs, so you can achieve your goals and become more successful, you need to reframe your perception of the benefits.

What will be the payoff—pain, or pleasure? Doing this involves changing two things: your emotions and your behavior. Focus on what you want and the feelings you nurture. How you feel influences your beliefs, and your beliefs become your actions. Let me take it further.

What you associate with pain determines your direction. The pain of success or the pain of mediocrity are two types of pain. The pain of working out, the pain of looking bad in your bathing suit, or on the dance floor, are other forms of pain. The pain of being alone or the pain of approaching a loved one and being rejected. All painful.

To have epic success, we must learn to attach and associate truckloads of pain to not acting and truckloads of pleasure to acting.

Remember your HISTEP from chapter four. This is where you can engage your motivational tools to create new beliefs. You can imagine all the fun you'll have for the rest of your life dancing at so many different places, trips, weddings, and social activities. You motivate yourself to take a few lessons. Now, when the opportunity to dance presents itself, you say to yourself, "I'm a good dancer, and I enjoy having fun." A new belief is born and nurtured.

You can also use your imagination in a negative way, and imagine you'll always be alone if you don't learn to dance because your mate will not want to be with someone boring and not willing to be playful. Therefore, taking a few dance lessons ensures you'll not live alone for the rest of your life! Trick your brain, or it will trick you.

When I used to do prospecting calls, I focused on the fact that my success would set me free financially. If that meant making 100 calls to make a $4,000.00 commission, I looked at it as making $40 for every call I made. $40 for every time I heard no. $40 for every person who hung up on me. I believed it.

Remember, trick your brain, or your brain will trick you! Don't believe me? How many times has your brain presented a scenario that you thought was true? Like "so and so is late because they don't care about me", or "they're cheating on me", or "they were in an accident", and it turned out to be false. You can be smarter than your brain.

A good friend and mentor of mine often tells himself he's feeling lucky. "Luck" often follows.

What are you telling (tricking) your mind into believing? Ask, and pull yourself back into the moment. Focus only on the moment, and make it a positive one.

It can be easy to fall into the trap of listening to the voices telling you not to call people because they are busy, they might be having dinner, and might hang up on you. Or maybe you zero in on the thought that cold-calling is hard work, or think about the times it hasn't worked in the past, believing it won't work now.

Don't listen to those voices. Change them, by saying, "That's an interesting, disempowering choice you're offering me." Tune into new, more positive thoughts. Try giving a name to the personality that's disempowering you, like Goofball, or Dopey. Then, just tell Dopey you're not into listening to him today.

If you're in sales, it's crucial to prospect and reach out to potential new clients to build your business. You know you need to connect with people. You also know there are people out there who want and need your services. When negative voices start up, remember belief is a feeling of certainty, based on fear or an illusion your mind creates to keep you safe. Don't let Dopey keep on talking and ruling your life.

Believe in yourself. Quiet the voices saying "I cannot", and just do it, like Roger Bannister, the man who broke the four-minute mile in running.

The accepted philosophy at the time, by doctors and athletes alike, was this milestone was not physically possible. Roger Bannister ignored all that. Each day, he focused on getting a little bit better and improving in very, very small increments. He focused on his goals, believed they were possible, and made it happen. Within one year, twenty other people repeated his feat! Now, they believed too, and they did it.

When somebody achieves something that once seemed impossible, other people think they can do it too. The new belief is installed in their operating system.

Limiting Voices in Your Mind

False assumptions: *They seem mean. She's mad at me and doesn't like me anymore. He's arrogant.*

Existential rationalizations: *It's not worth the effort. It won't work anyway. I'm not in the mood. I don't feel like it. I'm happy over here.*

Environmental doubt: *What will people think? What if they don't like me or approve of me? They're not my type.*

Self-doubt: *I don't know what to say. Last time, it didn't work, and that was embarrassing. I don't have enough time. I'm too old. I'm too young.*

If you're open to it, you can install any belief into yourself to achieve your goals and dreams, within reason. It's not reasonable to believe you can jump off a tall building and bounce back up like a rubber ball! But if you're committed and creative (because there will be blockages and obstacles along the way requiring creative solutions to work through), you can achieve just about anything.

As Henry Ford said, "Whether you think you can, or you think you can't, you're right."

Take a moment to look around. What tangible results of your life surround you in your home or office? What's your financial status? Look at your car, your house, your clothes, and your relationships. Everything you've created in your life. These are results based on decisions you made and actions you took based upon the beliefs you had.

What about your physical body? What results have you created in this department? Have you respected your body? Have you taken care of it? Or, do you struggle to get it to the place you want it to be?

Take a quick look at your relationships. Maybe your relationships, personal and professional, are the best part of your life. This could be an area in which you excel. If so, you have probably given them a great deal of attention and have strong beliefs surrounding other people and your ability to connect and bond with them.

On the other hand, some people struggle with relationships. They hold back in relationships, keeping everything nice and safe, and near the surface.

The results in your life come from the beliefs you have nurtured. Nurture beliefs that cause you to be empowered, that motivate you to do things that make you feel good, that get you great results in your life, and impact the world around you.

I encourage you to find the belief that will cause you to take action because that action will bring you rich results, making life more interesting and exciting.

Most people struggle with not wanting to make a mistake. So, they hesitate and over think things, racking their brains looking for all possible pitfalls before acting. This freezes them in a place of less or little action.

Since action is what gets results, you can be more successful than others by adopting the "say yes and figure it out later" belief we've discussed before (and that I'll get deeper into in my next book).

Remind yourself that when you give yourself a chance to make it happen—to be in the parade and not watching it pass you by, to be on the dance floor and not thinking about it on the sidelines—there is no losing. There is only losing the opportunity to live and learn.

By saying yes, you have a chance to live and be alive by doing. If you don't really know how you'll learn something, you'll figure it out by doing it. Win-win. Either you win or you learn. If you dance and look like a fool, you'll learn how to love yourself. Or you can face the fire of judgement and pain on the sidelines. Viewed this way, your resilience goes up each time you say yes, and it will be easier to handle more challenges in the future.

You can let your mind convince you to go with short-cut decisions called beliefs, or you can override your brain, and create a life of adventure and possibility. Keep reminding yourself of this key action you have control over, and keep saying yes.

By saying yes and figuring it out later, I'm an author. This is my second book. Before I began the process, I wasn't sure I could do it. But I jumped in and made it happen. I decided the reward was worth the pain of doing something new and scary.

Do you have a book in you that you believe you're not worthy to write? Do you want to do it, but tell yourself you don't have the time or worry your idea is not very good?

I believe we all have a book in us. We all have a story to tell that can benefit others. When is yours going to be real? Think about the thoughts holding you back (what I call "your story" about why you cannot do it). Then reach out to my coaches and partners, Full Sail Publishing. If you have a book in you, they'll help you get it written, edited, and published.

Most people know what to do, but they don't do it because fear stops them. Behind that fear is a limiting belief you can change. When you overcome limiting thought patterns, you'll be truly free.

Action Step

- **Pay attention. Monitor yourself. When you catch yourself saying something like, "I don't like working out. I don't have time to workout, and it doesn't make me feel good anyway," change it to, "I'm going to live longer, stronger, and every time I work out I get fired up, and I feel better. I love working out!" Learn to love challenging yourself, and you'll be amazed at the change.**

Confidence isn't an absence of fear but the ability to act despite the prospect of failure. We're usually not as nervous about things we've done before successfully. We know we're competent. The struggle comes in when we do something for the first time and confidence flees.

So how do you gain confidence about something you haven't done yet? You practice confidence; that's how.

Sound silly? Take a minute, right now, and think about what you'll be doing next. Then say, "I believe I can achieve anything when I'm committed and creative. I know if I'm committed, paying attention, and resourceful, something great is going to happen. I'm confident!" Remind yourself of the countless things you do every day without even thinking about them, things you learned through practice like walking, driving, brushing your teeth, or using a computer.

Practice saying yes anytime an opportunity presents itself. You're smart. You'll figure out how to deal with whatever comes along. It'll be exciting. You'll become inventive and, as you go through the experience, you'll start to become more confident. Having confidence will change your life.

Boost your confidence even more by acting as if you have done this (whatever this is) before. When your body starts to move, your brain will catch up. Just start doing it, and you'll improve as you go.

As Tony Robbins says, "The only thing holding you back from getting what you want is the story you keep telling yourself about why you can't have it."

You take care of certain things without hesitation. If you have children, you make sure they're fed and picked up from school. You don't leave them at school because you don't feel like going to pick them up. You can do anything you set your mind to with the right motivation and belief in yourself.

Get into the practice of thinking about your hot buttons (HISTEP). Go back, and review the section if necessary. Use your buttons to generate excitement and energy, to understand your setbacks, and use them to your advantage. Hot buttons generate momentum in your life. Believe your life will transform by using them, and it will.

Remember to maximize your downtime (like just before you go to sleep each night). Studies have shown the thoughts you have prior to going to sleep will be replayed throughout the night, planting seeds in your subconscious. We'll talk more about this later.

By now, you should be planning your schedule each week, spending a minimum of twenty-minutes every Sunday mapping out your goals and the action steps necessary to achieve them, and checking in with your progress and hot buttons. Ideally, you should have worked your way up to an hour of planning time every week, but even ten minutes will improve your chances of success.

Tonight, relive the highlights of your day before you lie down to go to sleep. Ask yourself what you learned, or achieved, and what you're grateful for. Let your conscious mind celebrate the successes you've had, and allow your unconscious to feel great about what you've achieved so far.

Use the power of your unconscious mind by programming it before you sleep. Let your brain work for you. As the French say, "*La nuit porte conseil*"—the night brings wisdom.

Action Steps

- **When you end your day, plant in your mind—pre-frame— your ideal upcoming day. Take a minute or two (perhaps while you're brushing your teeth) to think about tomorrow.**

> See yourself living it. Visualize, feel, hear, and see it. Know it's going to happen. Then, ask your unconscious mind to be completely prepared to make it happen the following day. Celebrate your upcoming success and then let it go.

- **When you have a problem you can't solve, before you go to bed, ask yourself how it can be solved. Ask your unconscious mind to guide you. Be open to all possibilities, and don't think on them now. Often, you'll wake up with the answer to your challenge. Don't force it. Don't fear it. Just ask. Then, let it go. Be relieved by that action alone, and know you'll be stronger for it.**

- **You may want to forgive yourself before you sleep and forgive some of the people in your life so healing can take place. You may ask for guidance in your life. You may ask yourself to overcome things that caused you pain throughout your day or you may talk with God. Just be sure to end on a positive note, and get a good night's sleep.**

Sleeping is essential for peace of mind and good health. Lack of sleep will cause irritation or depression. While you need a certain amount of sleep, don't overdose on it. Find out what works for you. Ask your body how much sleep it needs, and let it answer for you. You recharge as you sleep. Allow yourself to regain vitality and focus by ensuring you get the right amount of sleep. For most people, this is around seven or eight hours every night.

As you go to bed, expect to have a phenomenal night's sleep. Let go of your problems. They're not up to you anymore.

Wake up recharged and confident about the day to come.

Continually pay attention to how you feel, and focus on what you want in your life. Think about the outcome or payoff of meeting your goals. Dream about it. Use your imagination. Invest emotionally.

Stop being distracted by the other things sapping you of your energy, mission, vision, and obsession. Ditch TV, newspapers, gossip, and complaining. Just stop. Give those up. Trade them in.

Persistence will become easy because you'll be guided by what you love and by what you believe in most. It will be automatic, coded into your internal GPS system because you're operating from the programming of belief and persistence.

Repetition creates habits. Habits create beliefs that lead to our identity. All success and failures can be traced to what you do daily. What you do daily will build or destroy your identity.

Action Step

- **Try these empowering beliefs:**

I deserve the best in life.
I can have exactly what I want.
I make sure my most important needs are met.
I give myself what I really want and feel I deserve.
I'm giving life my passionate best effort.
Life is easiest when I create what I want.
I'm responsible for making the most of my life.
I take full responsibility for optimizing my thoughts, actions, and feelings.
I'm not a failure because I didn't get the result
I want; I'm a success because I gave it my
best effort.
When I hit frustration, I'm about to have a
breakthrough.
I give with the expectation that the universe
gives back.
Everything happens for a reason, and it serves us.
I can handle it. I'm enough. I'm worthy.

Three Things to Act on

Before completing the next step, look in a mirror and say: "I understand success comes from the implementation of knowledge, not the acquisition of it; therefore, I choose to step into an epic life by taking action on my new-found knowledge. As I read, I will capture the ideas that resonate with me and apply them to my life until I master them. Period. This is what badasses do, and I'm a badass. The result of these committed actions is an epic life!"

Action Step

- **Based on what you learned in this chapter, record three things in your journal or below that you're committed to acting on. Take as much space as you need to outline not only what you'll act upon, but how (steps you'll take), and the all-important why (your reason and result motivations and expectations). Write:**

I commit to take action on:

_____

_____

_____

_____

_____

_____

_____

_____

I commit to take action on:

_____

_____

_____

_____

_____

_____

_____

_____

I commit to take action on:

_____

_____

_____

_____

_____

_____

_____

_____

Chapter Six Recap

- Stop rationalizing.
  Stop criticizing.
  Stop complaining.
  Stop blaming.
- Replace limiting and crippling thought patterns by nurturing empowering beliefs.
- Feed and nurture your belief system, and focus on the results you want. Help yourself by working with a coach or an accountability partner who can act as a sounding board and keep you accountable.
- Identify your limiting beliefs. Remove them from your system like a pair of bad batteries, and install fresh ones.
- The pain of discipline is easier to deal with than the pain of regret.

Notes

CHAPTER SEVEN PREVIEW

Get a grip on your financial situation, and watch your net worth soar.

CHAPTER SEVEN

"Wealth is not about cash but more about cash-flow
from passive-income vehicles."
Rock Thomas

C hildren seem to work best when they have boundaries and routines, and so do most adults. Rituals and routines cause you to act
without over analyzing.

The more you develop the ability to act without overthinking, the
faster you'll move onward and upward.

Human beings are extremely programmable. There is a power
in repetition of habits, and anything repeated becomes part of your
everyday routine. The things you do today like taking a shower and
brushing your teeth will likely be repeated in the same fashion tomorrow.

Your failures can be traced to what you do or don't do daily. If you
overeat daily, you'll become fat. Do something wrong, and eventually,
there will be disaster. Do something right, daily, and there will be mir-
acles. Do small things each day, and you'll achieve incredible results.

The reason most people never tap into this power of the compound
effect (Darren Hardy's book *The Compound Effect* illustrates this very
well and is a must read), is due to something called "lag time".

Often, you don't feel the results of your choices until months or
years later. No immediate pain, no change in behavior! So, we have
the extra piece of cake. We say we will make that important call to-

morrow, imagining it will be easier, and we rationalize these actions by saying things like…it's only one piece, or just this time, or I never eat cake! We literally lie or trick our brains.

Or people say, "I don't drink," then add, "Well, I don't drink hard liquor, but an occasional glass of red wine is good for you."

I'm not saying people are lying on purpose. It's just so easy to trick ourselves when we don't understand the compound effect.

How do you know this is true? Play the opposite game. What if you eat that cake or muffin and it meant you'd get punched in the face, or you'd get arrested on the spot and put in jail for a night? What if not making that telephone call you promised yourself you'd make would mean your car was impounded for a month? What if you paid $100,000 to join a gym and every time you came in, they gave you $1,000 back?

Try it. Trick your brain so you're not swimming against the current of protection all the time.

Immediate feedback is lacking, so we don't value the small, incremental steps that lead to epic success. That must change if this is one of your habits.

If you have an area of your life where you have high pressure, you'll likely default to a certain pattern of behavior. The pathways in your brain have been carved and information channels have been created. The path you have travelled most will become your default under pressure.

You may have one of these patterns operating in your subconscious.

Look at your current financial situation. Do you work hard for the money you make? If you answered yes, then you probably have formed a belief that you must work hard for your money. Are you the type of person whose income goes up and down? Or, maybe you invest your money, then lose it, make some more, and do something else with it only to lose it again. If this is your pattern, you probably believe money is hard to keep and attract.

Action Step

- **What happened in the past is in the past. What matters now is what you do from this point forward. Try to catch yourself thinking thoughts that no longer serve you and replace them with new messages, messages supporting where you want to go today. Make these new, positive statements a habit, and carve new pathways in your subconscious.**

There are two types of habits: doing and not doing. Things you do in your day-to-day routine, you'll continue to do until you make a conscious decision to change your pattern. The same is true for things you're currently not doing. If you're in the habit of not balancing your checkbook, you'll continue not to do this until something happens causing you enough pain to make a change.

Most change comes about because of inspiration or desperation, a Triple EEE, or a moment of insight from an increased awareness about our programing. Desperation tends to kick in, resulting in tremendous pain or dire consequences when you fail in certain areas.

Doesn't it make more sense to act from a place of inspiration and move yourself to the path of least resistance? Don't you want to be motivated and rewarded by pleasure instead of punished and held back by the prospect of pain?

Your behaviors and approach to things like money will fall back to what's natural for you unless you make a conscious effort to change them. You can reprogram yourself for success just as easily as you can program yourself for failure.

In this chapter, I'll teach you three rituals to help you become financially free despite any limitations or negative programming you may be dealing with.

First, let's look at some different money-personality types:

Spenders: These people spend it as fast as they make it, usually to fill a hole caused by some emotional lack.

Savers/Hoarders: These people pinch every penny. It hurts them to spend money.

Avoiders: These people avoid the issue of money altogether, sometimes even refusing to look when they must pay for items at a cash register.

Money Monks: Monks believe money and spirituality don't mix and often self-sabotage their success.

It's hard to attract money if you're not comfortable with it, don't think about it, or are so afraid of losing it you can't bring yourself to spend it.

To be successful with your money, learn to view it the way wealthy people do. Just as you'll likely hang out with people you're comfortable with, money will too. It will go where it feels welcome.

Wealthy people don't measure their financial success by their salary or their income; they measure success by their net worth and cash flow from passive-income streams.

Action Steps

- **Calculate your net worth by taking the total of all you own (assets) and subtracting all you owe (debts). The resulting number is your net worth. And, yes, it's possible to have negative net worth. Knowing your net worth is the first step to gaining financial independence.**

- **Next, learn these four principles of wealth. Make them a part of your habits, and you'll be on the road to financial freedom:**

1. Pay yourself first (10% off the top of all incoming money).
2. Simplify your life.
3. Work within a budget.
4. Manage and invest your money.

If you're not following these principles, it's not because you can't; you're not in the habit of doing them.

Over 90% of people in North America who retire at the age of sixty-five, retire broke, in debt, or require some help from the government, their family, or friends. If you plan to live a long, strong life to the age of eighty or ninety-years-old, you're going to be in trouble if you don't have your finances worked out.

Consider this, the average NFL football player earns about 2.5 million dollars a year while they're playing, yet within two years of retiring, over 60% are bankrupt. Why? Because they didn't follow these four simple principles or focus on increasing their net worth. Like so many people, they focused on living in the moment, on instant gratification. They thought they could borrow from the future. Or maybe they didn't think about it at all.

People who become financially free look at money differently than 90% of the population. They look at making money to invest, while everyone else looks at money for lifestyle enhancement.

I'm going to share a simple strategy, so you can live a simple life, enjoy a nice standard of living, and at the same time be excited about your future.

If the idea of more rituals overwhelms you, try breaking the steps into small, bite-sized pieces. Baby steps. Take it one step at a time, aiming to spend about twenty minutes a day, five days a week tending to your financial well-being.

Action Steps

- **Pay Yourself First.**

Take 10% off the top of every dollar of income you make, and put it into a retirement account. Ignore the little voice in your head screaming it's not possible (but take note of it as we have discussed in previous chapters). The key is to do it automatically, so you don't even see it happening or have a chance to spend this money. Many employers will do this for you.

If you want an in depth understanding of "pay yourself first", read *The Richest Man in Babylon* by George Samuel Clason.

Consider this 10% a self-imposed tax you must pay all the time. When? All the time. No exceptions! Does the government say to you, "Oh, I noticed you're having a tough year. Let's skip paying taxes this year and check in next year when things are easier for you."? Crazy, right?

You need to treat your "pay yourself first" account in the same fashion. It's not negotiable.

The average North American spends 109% of what they earn (and growing, by the time this book is printed). We need to develop the habit of living off 90%. When you do, the 10% you put away will accumulate, and the magic of compound interest will help it grow over time, creating freedom for you and your family. There are many excellent resources available on setting up a savings plan. Find one that works for you.

If you're still thinking, "I don't have enough money. I can barely pay my bills as it is on what I earn!" start smaller. Find the place you feel comfortable with, and start there. The key is to develop the habit of saving. Start with a dollar or ten dollars each month if that's all you can truly do.

Open a savings account or retirement account. The action is what's important, not the amount. You're sending a message to the universe saying you're serious about developing this habit. When you send this message, an amazing phenomenon will occur. The universe will find ways to send you more money. Your spirit will become more open to receiving more money. Before you know it, your consciousness will be raised, and you'll start to do more, budget more, and experience money flowing your way more frequently. That's when things start to get exciting!

- **Simplify Your Life.**

There are always ways to simplify your life and reduce your expenses or increase your revenue.

Get creative. If you're committed and creative, there's always a way.

The more excited you are about something, the more tuned-in and conscious you become. Ignore any voices that pop up telling you saving a couple of dollars a month isn't going to get you anywhere (but take note of the voices, as always). As any kid with a lemonade stand can tell you, even pennies add up over time. Remember, it's the habits of the successful you're emulating at this point. Develop the habits, and the rest will follow.

- **Work Within a Budget.**

To become financially independent, treat your household budget and your household finances as if you were running a business.

IBM, Microsoft, and Apple have annual budgets. They report quarterly earnings, and they have a very tight measure of revenues, expenses, profits, and losses. When you work within a budget and treat your finances as a business does, you'll routinely measure what's going on in your financial domain. Pay attention to your stats, and get in the habit of paying cash for routine expenses.

Work within your budget. If you don't have the cash, you sacrifice or find an alternative you can afford, or you do without until you can save the money.

I highly recommend tools like Quicken software or Mint to help you develop a budget you can stick with. These systems will help you monitor and track expenses, income, and investments, and streamline everything you do involving your money.

Most people approach a budget by figuring out how much they make, how much they spend, and how much they want to invest or save. Others work backwards, and develop a monthly nut, or total of their monthly expenses, so they know how much they need to bring in the door each month. For me, it's more stressful to look at it that way. Why put any more pressure on yourself?

When you start to get clear about the bigger picture, and you understand the reasons why getting a handle on your finances is important, you'll find a way to implement a simple, yet powerful budget into your household.

Let's start with something easy. Calculate what you earned last year, and divide that number by 365. Now take all you spent, and divide that figure by 365.

Say you make $200 per day and spend $200 per day. But you need money to save. What are your options? You can increase your income by getting a raise, starting a part-time business, working overtime, or finding another way to take your income to $250 per day.

What if you reduce your expenses by making your own lunches, eating out less, and buying less unneeded "stuff". Would that reduce your expenses to $150 per day? Now, you have $100 per day to save! That's $36,500 in one year.

Wow! Small decisions = big results. We'll talk more about this later.

Remember, successful people are clear about the "why" behind their choices, and the "how" shows up.

More Money-Saving Ideas

1. Rent out a room, or buy a house and rent out several rooms.
2. Airbnb your home while you're on vacation or away for the weekend.
3. House swap for vacations.
4. Make your lunches on Sunday for the week.

5. Pick your clothes out for the week, and save time (time turns into money or freedom).
6. Stop buying things at 7-11. Think long term.
7. Vacation in third-world countries.
8. Take your bike, or walk instead of driving. Make it a fun goal to reduce your mileage by 15%–25% saving wear and tear on your car and gas money.
9. No lattes for a month.
10. Get Netflix, and cut your cable.
11. Get a second job, or start a business.
12. Learn about saving taxes (I know! Boring, but it pays well!).
13. Have a garage sale to get rid of things just sitting there, and take the $500 and invest it.
14. Car pool.
15. Wait an extra two weeks to get your hair cut and have a student do it.
16. Carry 'x' dollars in your wallet each week, and when nothing is left, you cannot spend more.
17. Work half a day on weekends.
18. Say yes to overtime.

- **Manage and Invest Your Money.**

The money you accumulate by paying yourself first is going to need to be managed and invested. I recommend you spend twenty minutes a day, five days a week working with your finances. Guess what? This is your new part-time job, and it will be for the rest of your life. Schedule this time on your calendar, and make it non-negotiable.

The more familiar you become with your finances (how you're doing with your budget and tracking your results) the more excited you'll become about your money situation. Your level of enthusiasm will grow, and your level of confidence and security will grow along with it. This may be a slow process at first when the numbers are smaller. But, in a very short period, you'll become energized by hundreds, then thousands, then tens of thousands of dollars building up in your accounts.

Even if you have very little, or no money, spending time learning about finance and various types of investments will benefit you.

Look at three key areas of investment options: Real Estate, Individual Stocks, and Mutual Funds.

Educate yourself in these arenas and consider Government Securities and Bonds as well. The returns on these types of investments may be smaller when compared to the stock market, but having a small, stable, guaranteed return vs losing money on riskier investments is a positive thing, especially when you're starting out.

It's easy to get frustrated and discouraged when your money is not growing or loses value, but the only way it will get any better is when you get educated on what makes money grow and what doesn't.

Set aside a small budget for investments each month. In my mastermind group, M1, we help you get better returns by introducing you to people who are doing it and having them walk you through each vehicle step by step.

The reason most people are never good at investing is due to a few factors.

90% of people never have savings to manage, so they never look at deals or get educated about investments until much later in life, and they generally suck at it.

They believe they must hit a home run to catch up for lost time. They might have messed it up in the past. They're jaded, bitter, and they hate wealthy people, driving them into ultra-conservative investments. They believe that wealth is for others and start late.

Wealth is created over time; it's not about getting rich with one great deal. That's a myth.

Many books, online courses, and seminars can provide the right tools for you to learn about money. M1 is just one of them. Some say ignorance is bliss, but when it comes to your business or finances, ignorance is expensive!

If you think you can farm out your financial well-being to a financial planner or manager that's certainly an option. They'll charge you a fee, and you'll have to over-see their activities.

Regardless of your choice, you must attend to this area of your life if you intend to enjoy financial success. There's no way around it. Respect money, and it will respect you.

Though it's not a very sexy topic, you should learn about taxes too. This may be the biggest area of opportunity to "find" hidden money for most people, especially if you're an employee.

Working with a professional in this area is a good idea. In the beginning, you may be able to handle your annual returns using a software program. As your net worth begins to grow and your investments become more diversified, having a professional to guide you is a must. In most cases, a good accountant and financial adviser can save you more than they cost. Unless you do these things for a living, you don't know what you don't know.

As with all investments of time into your development, focus on the benefits of educating yourself in these areas. The more you know, and are in touch with your finances, the more motivated you'll be to grow this critical area of your life and know exactly where you stand on major purchases and buying decisions. You'll also be more able to recognize a good financial opportunity when it comes along.

Still not convinced? Think about how many people know more about their car than they do about their body and how to take care of it. What's the result? They spend their health to gain their wealth, and later in life, they must spend their wealth to gain back their health, if they can.

Most of the world's population is struggling financially. Do you want to be one of the people who have figured out the money game, or do you want to be someone who struggles their entire life? That's easy to do. Just be one of the people who doesn't put away at least 10% of what they earn each month. Be one of the poor money managers who doesn't make saving a habit. Don't have a budget. Don't have any idea what's going on throughout the month with your money. Make all your decisions based on immediate gratification. When you're emotionally overwhelmed, go on a shopping spree to make yourself feel better instead of checking your needs, hot buttons, and goals, and coming up with a better way. And finally, make sure to live above your needs, rather than simplifying your life and investing the rest.

Make your financial matters a priority, and you'll never regret it. We live in a material world, and money is simply a measure of freedom. You work, put money to work for you, and you will have more freedom.

If you make barely enough to survive, you'll have to work the next day, and the next, and the next. But if you learn what I teach in my "March to a Million" mastermind group (M1), you'll understand that one must first master oneself to take action in any area. You'll master money so it goes to work for you every day. Then, you'll master leading others by building a vision and getting others to work for you.

Financially free people—the richest people in the world—have others doing "stuff" for them like cleaning their cars, houses, shopping, booking flights, and a million other tasks, so they can do things that make the real money. Usually, they've had a period in their life when they lived below what they earned, so they could put extra money to work for them.

The person who makes $200 a day and spends $250 is borrowing it from who? The guy who make $250 and lives off $200 makes interest off the money he loans to the poor individual who has not learned what you're learning here.

Credit cards make most of their money off people who cannot pay their monthly bill, and interest rates are generally high. 18%–27%! Are you kidding me?

I pay off my credit card every month without fail. Yet, many people don't have emotional mastery, and the big companies know this, so they're the ones getting wealthy off consumers' lack of education or understanding about the impact of their emotional, impulsive decisions.

Don't be like those people. Get your shit together, and get on the road to financial freedom.

Three Things to Act on

Before completing the next step, look in a mirror and say: "I understand success comes from the implementation of knowledge, not the acquisition of it; therefore, I choose to step into an epic life by taking action on my new-found knowledge. As I read, I will capture the ideas that resonate with me and apply them to my life until I master them. Period. This is what badasses do, and I'm a badass. The result of these committed actions is an epic life!"

Action Step

- **Based on what you learned in this chapter, record three things in your journal or below that you're committed to acting on. Take as much space as you need to outline not only what you'll act upon, but how (steps you'll take), and the all-important why (your reason and result motivations and expectations). Write:**

I commit to take action on:

_____

_____

_____

_____

_____

_____

_____

_____

I commit to take action on:

_____

_____

_____

_____

_____

_____

_____

_____

I commit to take action on:

_____

_____

_____

_____

_____

_____

_____

_____

Chapter Seven Recap

➢ Your behavior and approach to things like money will fall back to what's natural for you unless you make a conscious effort to change them. You can program yourself for success just as easily as you have already been programed for failure, mediocrity, getting a job, and retiring. These are flawed methods to living an epic life that I don't endorse or encourage.

➢ Learn these rituals of the rich, make them a part of your habits, and you'll be on the road to financial freedom:

> *Pay yourself first*
> *Work within a budget*
> *Simplify your life*
> *Manage and invest your money*

➢ Many books, online courses, and seminars can provide the right tools for you to learn about money. Some say ignorance is bliss, but when it comes to your business or finances, ignorance is expensive! Educate yourself.

➢ Find an online budgeting course or program that will help you create your budget. Once you start a budget, make sure to schedule time (a minimum of once per week) to update and review your budget. What gets measured gets managed, and what you manage grows.

➢ The book *Secrets of the Millionaire Mind: Mastering the Inner Game of Wealth* by one of my mentors, T. Harv Eker, is a foundational book that every epic man and woman should read.

CHAPTER EIGHT PREVIEW

Nothing changes in life until a daily routine is changed. Do these things and you'll have a physical, mental, and emotional edge on your competition. You'll hit the day running, full of energy and determination. The purpose of your morning and evening rituals is to set and reset your internal vibration higher to attract its equivalent, to put you into a beautiful state of mind, and increase your energy level, allowing you to experience the best day possible.

Chapter Eight

Rule Eight: Success is a ritual. It's not owned;
it's leased. You pay the rent every day
with your efforts.

*"You'll never change your life until you change
something you do daily."*
John C. Maxwell

What successful people do first thing in the morning (before eight o'clock) and what they do after eight o'clock at night, is something that separates them from average individuals.

I've studied the most successful, happiest, most peaceful, powerful, magnetic, charismatic, and consistent people on the planet for twenty-five years. Without exception, they've found success comes from a repeatable daily routine.

In this chapter, I'll share some of the rituals and habits we use that will help you create the epic life you want, giving you the advantage over your unconscious ways. More than ever, these tools are needed as social media and our mobile devices are constant mental distractions.

Do these things, and you'll have a physical, mental, and emotional edge on your competition. You'll hit your day running rather than reeling. Science has determined that you'll be less stressed and happier when you follow these suggestions.

Action Step

- **Take a minute to reflect on your average morning ritual. What's it like? What's the first thing you do when you wake up? What do you do for the first couple of hours before the day gets going?**

If I don't get a good start to my day by the time it's nine o'clock, I feel stressed out. I'm already on the defense. I'm reacting. I've not had a chance to center myself, to visualize what I'm about to create or experience in my day. I've not had time to do any of the things we've talked about so far.

Let's recap things you could be doing:

- ✓ Thirty-minutes a day of reading, learning, or listening to motivational stories on YouTube or Podcasts
- ✓ Setting or reviewing your goals and activating your RAS
- ✓ Doing something you love, if you're not already doing it as your passion or career
- ✓ Thinking about how to use HISTEP to motivate and activate your drive and actions
- ✓ Visualizing, meditating, and imagining your focused energy at work
- ✓ Doing incantations to drive away limiting beliefs, and nurture the strong ones
- ✓ Managing and overseeing your finances

If you haven't had time to take care of yourself or meet many of your needs at this point in the book, ask yourself why. Take some time to get on track, and read *The Miracle Morning* for inspiration. Even if you read it when I suggested it earlier, it's worth a review to add new tools to your toolbox.

The best way to start your day, as soon as you open your eyes, is to say something positive. "It's going to be a great day," is perfect, though what you say is not as important as the ritual of saying the positive statement and checking in with how you feel about what you say.

It's important to do this within moments of waking up. Don't wait for a few minutes, or until after you've had a chance to review the swirl of things on your mind.

If you went to bed feeling stressed out about a project or situation, it will probably be one of the first things that pops into your head in the morning. The negative energy surrounding many of these thoughts will make you feel anxious and stressed. Replace negative thoughts with positive messages to set the tone for your day from the very first moment. Make it a ritual.

Sometimes, I'm tempted to stay in bed when my alarm rings because I'm tired. However, I always get up, and I always get up earlier than most people do. I know if I hit snooze a few times, I'm setting myself up for a negatively-charged morning that will carry over into my day. It's like setting a goal to get up at a certain time and then failing each time you hit the snooze button. Why do that to yourself?

This is what I say as soon as I wake each morning: "It's going to be an amazing day, filled with magical moments I create and the universe creates for me. I will treat people with kindness and respect by being playful and passionate. I'm open and grateful for this day and appreciate the ride, the surprises, and the gifts. I'm committed fully to the practice of a beautiful state of mind and will achieve it through meditation. I'm fully committed to living the practice of the top-ten rules to have an epic life. I'm committed to fully living a life of abundance through a mindset that doesn't include the limiting thoughts of comparison, competition, judgement, and criticism, with the desired intention to feel better by putting others down. Rather, I choose to be the best version of me in all situations."

When I catch myself judging someone, I complete the sentence by saying "just like me" to bring awareness to what I'm projecting out and remind myself that's not about the person I'm judging but merely my filters responding to outside stimulus.

Action Step

- **Repeat after me "Today will be the best day of my life, and I will live it as though it's a gift from my creator and do my very best to make all those I meet feel loved, connected, and appreciated."**

You should also go to bed on a positive note, reviewing the goodness of your day, setting yourself up for a restful night's sleep. Saying something like, "Today has been a great day, and tomorrow will be even better," will put yourself into a positive frame of mind.

Start and end your days on the same positive note.

Journaling is a helpful way to remember the highlights of your day. You might find *The Five-Minute Journal: A Happier You in 5 Minutes a Day* useful.

Capture your day in writing. Make these statements out loud too, not just in your mind, as you write or think about them in the morning and at night. Declare them, loud and proud, as this makes a difference to your mind and in your subconscious when they hear your declarations made with power and authority.

Successful people start from the inside out. They get up and declare something positive. They take care of their bodies, and they focus on what they want to create emotionally throughout their day as soon as they wake up. In short, they manage their inputs.

Struggling people reach for their phone before they're out of bed and start reacting to other people's agendas. They turn on the television or radio when they wake. They start surfing the latest news and gossip on the internet or reading the newspaper within the first few minutes after getting up.

Instead of filling their heads with something energizing and positive, reading the newspaper or watching the news exposes us to largely negative stories and information which affect us emotionally. Before you know it, you feel sad or mildly depressed and carry those feelings with you throughout the morning.

If you're thinking that having a little input for your mind before bedtime is a good thing, let me remind you that your brain is always looking for ways to protect you. If you see someone say you shouldn't invest in a stock or real estate and you were about to do this, your brain must manage that scary thought.

Let's say you turn on the TV and see the stock market hit an all-time high, and the "experts" are worried it's about to "correct". Your brain will say, "Maybe he is right." Or let's say you're thinking of buying real estate, and your brain is looking for evidence to protect you. All this worry can create a sleepless night and distract you from your goals.

Manage your inputs. Be smart about what you allow in. Know that television has one job to do—sell air time. Advertisers and the media use fear to impact our thoughts and buying habits. Even a broken clock will be right twice a day, and eventually a market correction will happen, but you might live in fear, doubt, and worry for years until it happens.

Manage your investments on your schedule, and forget about them the rest of the time.

Action Step

- **Go on a news "fast". Try it for a week.**

When I was running my real estate company, I watched sales people come in around 9:30 or 10:00 with cobwebs in their head, looking like they were just trying to get going.

Successful people don't start their day at 10 o'clock in the morning. They start early, and they get a jump on their days. By mid-afternoon, they've finished their work, and earned the rest of the day off. They can schedule days off and work hard to accomplish their weekly goals, so when it comes time to stop working, they enjoy their leisure time peacefully as they've earned it.

Successful people are also usually fit people. They take care of their bodies as well as their minds. They don't skip breakfast. Nutritional experts agree breakfast is the most important meal in the day. After fasting for seven or eight hours during our sleep, your body is ready for nutrition to get moving. Just like with a car, the greatest amount of energy is needed to get started and pull away from the garage. Once you get going, momentum takes over, and your energy requirements are much less.

Here are some other easy-to-adopt behaviors I learned from my mentors with exceptionally high levels of energy and huge amounts of results in their lives:

Nourishment and Alkalinity: Drink at least eight ounces of water first thing in the morning with a squeeze of real lemon juice. Take a lemon, quarter it the long way, and leave the pieces in a container in your fridge, so you can easily grab a quarter and squeeze it into your water glass. Lemon helps activate your digestive system and prepare your stomach to digest your breakfast. Skip the lemon if you're opposed to the taste, but get in the habit of drinking water before you start eating food or drinking coffee.

Motion Creates E-Motion: Get moving immediately in the morning. Jump out of bed; don't linger. You should be working out three days a week (minimum). Walking is fine, and you can do it anywhere. Do some stretching to loosen up your muscles and joints. Listen to some great music, and get yourself fired up. I sometimes do "chaotic dance" which is moving my body in a way that has no rules—like an excited six-year-old who just learned they're going to Disney World, allowing myself to move and be free. Remember, we're emotional beings, so if you cannot start to direct your emotions, you won't be at your optimal state of being.

Have fun!

Incantations or Affirmations: Successful people focus on what they want to create when they workout. They talk to themselves in a positive and energizing way about their goals and their emotional state. By using autosuggestions, you can reinforce your beliefs and help solidify them within your subconscious mind. I said, "I'm the greatest real-estate agent in the world, and people want to do business with me!" when I worked out during my most successful period as a realtor.

What are your autosuggestions like in the morning? Be honest. Are you saying, "It's a great day," or something like, "I hate Mondays."?

You may have responsibilities like preparing your children for school. Getting up earlier may seem difficult at first, but giving yourself this quiet time to build yourself from the inside out will center and focus your energy. Everything you do will seem easier when you've taken care of yourself first.

Improve a skill or learn something new: When I wrote my first book, I did my writing early in the morning and late at night. I took a typing course online for twenty minutes a day for several months. I went from typing twenty words a minute to sixty or seventy words a minute. This total transformation of my typing skills allowed me to type faster and complete my writing goals in less time and with less frustration.

Think about what skills you need to sharpen. Is it possible to work on these skills for a few minutes in the morning or later in the evening? A small investment of time for a few weeks could be a huge step in moving ahead with your projects. It will certainly eliminate any excuses you may be using to hold yourself back.

Meditation: Over 1000 recent studies have shown that meditation has many benefits that can no longer be ignored. I've adopted a few different styles of meditation that include directed thoughts and others focusing solely on breathing methods. If you'd like some options, go to YouTube, search for meditation, and learn about your choices.

Gratitude and forgiveness are powerful benefits that go hand in hand with meditation. These two things alone will transform your life dramatically. In the book *The Code of the Extraordinary Mind* by Vishen Lakhiani, there's a six-phase meditation that's one of my favorites.

Imagination and visualization: Spending time thinking about what you want is important and is opposite to what scientists have proven most people do. Why? Because we're genetically set up to search for things that might hurt us (our reptilian brains at work again). We've already discussed the many ways more positive programming will impact your life for the better. The trick is to do it.

Action Step

- **Use your journal or the space below to list a skill you'll work on and how you'll do it (be specific).**

_____

_____

_____

_____

_____

_____

_____

We're given the same amount of time in our days. We all have responsibilities. You can make the most of your time, and your day, if you get a jump on the rest of the world and use this extra time to better yourself and move faster toward your goals.

Your goal should be to integrate as many different strategies from these rules as possible into your life, from the moment you get up in the morning to the moment you go to bed at night.

Action Steps

- **Use autosuggestions on readily available audio programs and podcasts to crystallize your beliefs and reinforce your positive behaviors.**

- **Recite what you learn in the shower and car, and repeat the thoughts you wish to experience.**

- **Practice pushing some of your hot buttons to create a sense of urgency about an important goal. Use exaggeration in this process and reflect on a Triple E to magnify the motivational elements.**

- **Listen to personal development programs instead of the news in the morning or while you drive to work.**

- **While working out, focus on your self-talk. Workout, not only physically, but mentally and emotionally too.**

Working on a specific skill will unlock your true potential and help pave the way to hitting future goals faster and more efficiently. We live in a fast-changing world, and your success will depend on how you evolve. If you don't have a systematic strategy to improve as part of your routine, evolution won't occur.

If you find yourself struggling with sleep and feeling tired all the time, one of two things is most likely the cause. Either you're not taking care of your body, with regular exercise and a healthy diet, or you're struggling with things like stress or worry caused by a lack of strategies to overcome your situation.

You're Either Growing or Dying. There is No in Between.

We're dying from the moment we're born. To achieve personal growth throughout our lives, we must put in a little extra each day to overcome the constant force of aging. It's easy to sit back, do nothing each day, and go with the flow. Unfortunately, if you're passive, you'll fall behind. Therefore, I strongly suggest you have routines and regularly developed habits that cause you to be your best.

To be successful, if we do what the most successful people do (the smartest strategy), then we're going to take advantage of what we choose to do before 8:00 in the morning and what we do after 8:00 at night to live an epic life. If you're working from 9:00 to 5:00 and you want to open your own business or have a sideline business, you're going to have to start working on it when everyone else is sleeping or sitting in front of the TV.

Most people can manage to stumble to a job during the day or push themselves to accomplish something while others appear to be fired up with the energy of working. However, what you do behind closed doors, and before and after hours, is often what makes the difference.

When you have a compelling future and you have RRAFTed, you tend to be excited about your life. Sleep becomes less important. Putting things in your body that slow you down becomes less tempting. You spend your days fired up about creating, experiencing, and giving back. When you spend time in the margins (before 8:00 and after 8:00), doing things that are educational or increase your net-worth, you're fast-tracking to success. Remember, when you're not out gallivanting but instead spending time working on building your dreams, your brain, or your body, you're not spending money either, which doubles your speed toward financial freedom. Win, win!

Increase the richness in your life. Make yourself rich in energy. Rich in happiness and rich in results. Make these habits something you do every single day. Develop a whole-life-wealth mentality.

Rich and successful people talk to themselves in a positive manner. They remind themselves of their "big whys" when they get up early or stay up late. They speak in the present tense as if what they're pursuing has already happened. It's a done deal. They don't say, "I'm going to be a great father or husband one day." They say, "I'm a great dad." When people ask them how they're doing, they don't say "fine" or "good". They say "fantastic", "great", "grateful", or "phenomenal"! These may seem like small things, maybe even a little silly, but they really make the difference between feeling good and feeling great. Words have the power to empower you or disempower you.

Autosuggestions and self-talk are stimuli that appeal directly to our neurology and feelings. The stronger the feelings, the more successful the outcome will be. Suggestions need to appeal to your imagination, not the analytical, logical, reasoning, side of your brain. They must stir emotions within you to provide energy and reinforce beliefs. There must be that component of belief or the process won't work.

If you were to say, "I'm the greatest real-estate agent in Montreal," but you don't really believe it, then you're not going to resonate with that belief or attract the components necessary to have it in your life. You may even talk yourself out of trying.

This is probably the defining and most critical component of all successes—you need to believe you deserve success, that you're worthy of it, and believe it's coming to you. We are what we do emotionally. We *do* emotions and beliefs. They don't *do* us.

You can learn to create positive emotions by focusing on them consistently. Reflect on times when you felt great, and reenact these experiences in your mind.

As we've discussed, doing this before bed and first thing in the morning sets you up for positive thinking and, over time, this pattern will be programmed into your thought processes. What you say to yourself must be positive, believable, and regular. It requires a lot of repetition. Throughout this process, imagine and visualize the result you desire as real.

Focus on the future, not the past. Use the past as a resource of information, so you can become enriched by it, not impoverished. Ask yourself better questions. Focus on solutions and opportunities for improvements, not problems. Focus on the possibilities and what will be.

Jim Carrey wrote himself a ten-million-dollar check prior to becoming famous. He told everyone he met that he was the funniest man in Hollywood and said one day he would cash that check. Each day, he would practice for several hours, making funny faces in the mirror, reinforcing his belief in who he was. Sure enough, a few years later, he cashed that check, two weeks before the date he had written on it.

Having a burning desire to accomplish a goal provides an amazing side benefit—a shield to deflect the negativity and naysayers of the world. Some great success stories of people who overcame major odds and achieved success are Sylvester Stallone, Arnold Schwarzenegger, Oprah Winfrey, and Meryl Streep. These people came from nothing and became successful because they had a clear vision and gave themselves an edge by working on their inner game before 8:00 in the morning and after 8:00 in the evening.

You may give your 9:00 to 5:00 to someone else, but if you give up your before 8:00 and after 8:00 to anything else, like surfing social media or entertainment news, then you may find yourself not being intentional or purposeful (and wasting a lot of time).

Successful people make things easier on themselves by leveraging the power of ritual and routine. They avoid over thinking.

One of my mentors, a successful businessman, doesn't have to think about reading three papers on international business every day. The habit's automatic. He doesn't think about whether he should have a drink at lunch or not. He has a rule that says he doesn't drink alcohol. He stays more alert and has a couple of extra hours a day in maximum energy mode.

Ask yourself what better rules and rituals you can add to your daily routine and into your life. If you're having trouble making this shift (or giving up some of the vices in your life—some "old friends" that are holding you back), then go back to chapter four and have a look at your emotional hot buttons and triggers. The vehicles you're using may not be serving you.

I too once had many vices and made poor choices that didn't serve me. But I changed, and so can you.

Find a different, better, more productive vehicle to get you engaged without relying on food, alcohol, drugs, or television to get you through the day. Change your perspective to include clear pictures of what achieving your goals will do for your self-esteem, your sense of security, your family, your children, and their future. The clearer these pictures are the better. Post them on your dream board, on your desk, on your bathroom mirror, in your car, and anywhere you can be reminded of them and energized.

These routines need to become automatic, until you execute them at a level of unconscious competence, where you can do them with your eyes closed. You'll no longer waste time wondering what you should do. You'll already know.

Start tomorrow. Get up earlier, and take on the day with a routine that will serve you well.

You're working on yourself from the inside out. You're focused on what you want, what you want to create, and what you want to experience in your day. You will become centered and strong all day.

Three Things to Act on

Before completing the next step, look in a mirror and say: "I understand success comes from the implementation of knowledge, not the acquisition of it; therefore, I choose to step into an epic life by taking action on my new-found knowledge. As I read, I will capture the ideas that resonate with me and apply them to my life until I master them.

Period. This is what badasses do, and I'm a badass. The result of these committed actions is an epic life!"

Action Step

- **Based on what you learned in this chapter, record three things in your journal or below that you're committed to acting on. Take as much space as you need to outline not only what you'll act upon, but how (steps you'll take), and the all-important why (your reason and result motivations and expectations). Write:**

I commit to take action on:

_____

_____

_____

_____

_____

_____

_____

_____

I commit to take action on:

_____

_____

_____
_____
_____
_____
_____
_____
_____

I commit to take action on:

_____
_____
_____
_____
_____
_____
_____

Keep a Daily Journal Challenge

Taking up a new habit takes time and repetition.

Action Step

- **For the next seven days, write about your day in a journal. At the end of the week, read about your experiences, and note how rewarding it is to capture them on paper.**

Chapter Eight Recap

"The first hour of the day is the rudder of the day."
Henry Ward Beecher

- ➢ Develop daily routines.
- ➢ Wake up, and declare, "It's a great day!" aloud. It is a fantastic day simply because you woke up. Every day you open your eyes is a great day, right?
- ➢ Hydrate yourself by drinking water when you wake (at least eight ounces). Add some fresh-squeezed lemon to get your digestive system firing on all cylinders.
- ➢ Get your energy flowing early by moving, stretching, and exercising.
- ➢ Motivate yourself with self-talk and autosuggestions, focusing on what you want to create in your life. Whatever it is for you, repeat it. Repetition will drive these messages deep into the cells of your body and transmit that energy to the universe. You'll become a magnet for things you want to attract, and your clarity and declarations will help manifest them in your life.
- ➢ Before you fall asleep at night, get centered and strong. Pull from the quietness of the universe to connect with what's important for you. Visualize your life, exactly the way you know it will be. Tell yourself it already is this way. Do this again first thing in the morning.
- ➢ Be conscious and clear about where you want to go and what you're going to focus on. Remember, you are what you eat, you are what you think, and you are what you do repeatedly, so take ownership of these things starting today. These new "rules" are designed to help you create an awesome day, a beautiful week, a fantastic month, and an amazing year.

Notes

CHAPTER NINE PREVIEW

*Develop the ability to look at things in several
different ways, and choose the ones that best
serve you as you pursue your goals.*

CHAPTER NINE

Rule Nine: Become a master of meaning.

"Nothing in life has any meaning until you give it meaning."
Tony Robbins

Judgment, perception, and our take on things based on experience, creates our reality. If you say it's so, then it is. If you believe it, then it's true. It's not a lie, if you believe it. It's not what happens to you, it's how you choose to respond that makes a world of difference.

Many years ago, a man named W. Mitchell was involved in a motorcycle accident and was burned over a large part of his body. He spent years in the hospital getting skin grafts, and undergoing many painful surgeries and grueling physical therapy sessions. Many people would have checked out, given up. But, he didn't quit until he became better.

He opened a business and obtained his private pilot license. Flying with his buddies one day, his plane crashed. Everybody walked away from the accident except for him. He was paralyzed from the waist down. Against all odds, he had suffered two major traumatic events within a very short period.

At this point, your mind might be reeling a bit. Pay attention to the thoughts you're having. Do you believe these events just randomly happened to W. Mitchell, or do you think he was in control of his life, his situation, and his destiny, and that everything was exactly as it was supposed to be?

W. Mitchell decided to focus on what he knew he could control. He adjusted his focus and today says, "Before my accidents, there were ten thousand things I could do. After the accidents, there were only nine thousand I could do. When I focused on the thousand I could not do anymore, I felt depressed. But when I focused on the nine thousand I could still do, I felt good. I wanted to feel good. I think everybody wants to feel good and be happy. I focused on that." Mitchell decided to focus on the nine thousand things he could still do and ask better questions. Instead of asking why these things had happened to him, he asked what he could do now. He asked himself, "How great is my life today? What can I learn from this?"

He went on to marry the nurse who took care of him! How cool is that? He could have thrown in the towel; instead, he ended up running for political office using the slogan "Not just another pretty face". Amazing!

My teacher from India, Anandagiri (some might say my spiritual guide or teacher), says that all suffering comes from being self-centered and focusing on what's missing or on what should be or could be rather than living from a sense of appreciation for what is and contributing to making other peoples' lives better.

Children have an incredible ability to look at the positive in a situation. Looking at things in a negative light is a learned behavior. A child can look at the backyard and see all the pretty, colorful flowers, while their parents will look at the same yard and see all the weeds taking over and the grass begging to be mowed.

Start consciously developing new perspectives and look for more than one meaning in every situation. Don't simply give in to your default mode all the time, locked into tunnel vision.

It takes practice, and it takes conscious effort to develop new ways of thinking. It takes energy to carve out new neural pathways in your brain, like building muscles at the gym. It's not going to happen overnight, just as getting your body in shape doesn't happen after only one or two workouts.

When a major emotional event takes place in your life, especially a negative one, you'll go through five phases. Let's walk through them.

Shock. I can't believe this happened. Your mind races to catch up with what you're seeing and experiencing. Mostly, you'll be in disbelief.

Anger, which often lasts for days, weeks, even lifetimes for many people who're stuck here. If you cannot get past this one, ask yourself why you're so angry. Don't try to mute your feelings by smothering them with food, drugs, alcohol, television, gossip, or some other distraction. Rather, find a process to start letting go of the debilitating emotion of anger.

Rationalizing. In this phase, we attempt to negotiate or compromise after the fact. If you or someone close to you were to get sick, have an accident, or be near death, you might try negotiating with God, a Doctor, or the authorities in control. In all cases, it's usually too little, too late because the result or event has already happened.

Sadness, pain, and sorrow is the stage when you realize there's nothing you can do. You lost the sale. You had the car accident. Somebody passed away. During this phase, you may experience depression. The danger of this phase is possibly losing the capacity to navigate yourself out of it without help. How long you spend here will determine the quality of your life. The difficulty of picking up the ball again increases with time spent in this funk.

Acceptance is the final phase. Think about an event or situation you went through in your life that was either traumatic or highly emotional. Isn't it true that at some point you accepted what hap pened? Successful people are not just optimistic. They don't simply have a good attitude and focus on positive things. They realize there is more than one perspective in every situation, often factors beyond their control, that they need to let go of.

Acceptance and the ability to let go of things beyond their control is what often separates successful individuals from those who are stuck in a rut.

The most successful people can snap out of it, rebound, pick themselves up, and use their energy. They channel it to fire themselves up the same way W. Mitchell did. The same way Michael Jordan still does. The same way all successful people do. The way you're doing now, reading this book and reframing your life in a positive and energizing way.

Successful people believe they make life happen and that life is not happening to them. They believe they are responsible for everything in their lives—successes, victories, challenges, failures, good, bad, insert any label you wish.

Do you take full responsibility for everything in your life? Take a minute to think about it. It's a great question and can spark extremely powerful emotions which create action. It's all good.

Let's run a typical situation through the five stages. Suppose you get stopped for speeding by a police officer.

Your first reaction might be "Oh, my gosh, I can't believe it! I was barely speeding. Darn, I didn't see him there. I don't believe this is happening." Then you start to think about how much this is going to cost you, and you start to think about what else you could have done with that money, and you get angry.

When the police officer approaches the window, you attempt to negotiate. "Officer, what did I do wrong? Please, listen. I'm in a rush. I didn't see the signs, and the speed limit's ridiculous here. Nobody drives that speed. You know that." In most cases, your excuses are to no avail. So, you move on to sadness. Your shoulders slump. You want to call a friend and share your sadness. "You won't believe what happened to me!" You may even return to anger for a while until, ultimately, you go to acceptance. "Oh well, it is what it is. At least I didn't get caught going faster." And, hopefully, you let it go and move on.

Some people like to stay stuck in their drama and tell the story over and over. They get angrier, fight the law, or write a letter to the editor, and they stay in anger mode or refuse to pay, and go to court trying to negotiate. These are all choices you make. I'm merely pointing out that most successful people rapidly process these emotions, learn the lessons, and move on to acceptance while learning and becoming empowered by everything that happens in their lives.

If you're struggling, you may find yourself resisting these changes. You may do the exact opposite. You may think life is something that happens to you and is out of your hands. Shit happens. There's nothing I can do about it.

Have you ever dealt with a customer service agent who said something like, "Unfortunately, there is nothing I can do."? This type of thinking frustrates me as these people have been programed to look for what cannot be done. I hope that's not you.

Are you success oriented or victim oriented? There is always something you can do. Believe it. Even if what you do is learn or see something you can appreciate in the moment.

Losing to an opponent means you can appreciate how well they performed in the moment. Acknowledging your own potential means your day is just around the corner.

Beliefs are not true or false. They are not right or wrong. They are only empowering or disempowering.

Successful people own the results in their life. They create them. They make changes and course corrections to improve their results anytime they have a setback.

Taking responsibility means you own everything that happens to you. It means you believe you're the cause of all your results.

You may be familiar with these cause and effect rules:

For every action, there is an equal and
opposite reaction.
You never get something for nothing.
You'll get as good as you give.
What goes around, comes around.

When you own your results, your success and your failures, you'll be motivated to draft a blueprint designed to help you achieve great things.

The only place success comes before work is in the dictionary. Once you have your plan, you must execute it. You must make sure you have the proper tools in your toolbox to handle anything getting in the way of reaching your goals.

Look at people who get results in their lives, like Stephen Covey, or Will Smith, or Mark Zuckerberg, and you'll see they all found tools to help keep them on track when the going got tough. These tools vary just like a carpenter's tools would be different from a painter's. The successful person develops the ability to choose from a variety of tools and takes full responsibility for what they produce with them.

Struggling people believe life happens to them—the economy is holding them back, their boss has power over them, the hours they must work are not their choice. They hope and pray they will have a good day and wish things could be different. At the end of the day, what all struggling people seem to have in common is they don't feel in control of their life.

To master the meaning in your life, and be in control, ask yourself better questions. Questions create focus.

One of my favorite questions is, "What's great about this?" When I ask myself that question, it causes me to focus on the positive in all situations. You'll find when you shift your perspective, even slightly, you can see a situation from a different point of view.

Action Step

- **Ask yourself these questions, and use your journal to record your answers or record them below:**

What's my greatest asset?

_____

_____

What would be most profitable for me to be involved in?

_____

_____

What would I enjoy doing the most?

_____

_____

Who is the most important person in my life?

_____

_____

Who do I most want to work with?

_____

_____

Who is the best person to speak to about a problem I'm having?

_____

_____

When is the best time of day for me and why?

_____

_____

When am I most productive?

_____

_____

What am I best at?

_____

_____

What's the best thing about my relationships?

_____

_____

Where is my best source of inspiration?

_____

_____

What's the best restaurant in the city?

_____

_____

What was great about today?

_____

_____

What do I like and admire most about myself?

_____

_____

What are my favorite things to do?

_____

_____

What would make each task today more pleasurable?

_____

_____

What's the best solution to my problems and concerns?

_____

_____

What can I do to bring about the best in myself and others?

_____

_____

Optimal people are always looking for the best. Build yourself a list of questions that will allow you to be the best possible thinker for every situation you're in, knowing choices are going to be yours to make. Give yourself a default program you can go to at an unconscious level.

Your experience in life depends on the decisions you make and the internal representations you create through your thoughts and actions. If you're not getting the results you want, change the picture you have of your future, and take ownership over your thoughts and actions by changing whom you spend time with, what you read, and how you talk with yourself and your friends.

Ask yourself, "What's working? What's not working?" Most people tend to look at the problem (what's not working) and not the solution. Stop focusing on the problem, and focus on the solution! Stop living in the past and fearing the future. Live in the present, and focus on what you can do right now to reach your goals.

Three Things to Act on

Before completing the next step, look in a mirror and say: "I understand success comes from the implementation of knowledge, not the acquisition of it; therefore, I choose to step into an epic life by taking action on my new-found knowledge. As I read, I will capture the ideas that resonate with me and apply them to my life until I master them. Period. This is what badasses do, and I'm a badass. The result of these committed actions is an epic life!"

Action Step

- **Based on what you learned in this chapter, record three things in your journal or below that you're committed to acting on. Take as much space as you need to outline not only what you'll act upon, but how (steps you'll take), and the all-important why (your reason and result motivations and expectations). Write:**

I commit to take action on:

_____

_____

_____

_____

_____

_____

_____

_____

_____

I commit to take action on:

_____

_____

_____

_____

_____

_____

_____

_____

_____

_____

_____

I commit to take action on:

_____

_____

_____

_____

_____

_____

_____

_____

_____

CHAPTER NINE RECAP

➢ Become a master of meaning by becoming aware of the meaning you attach to things and events in your life.

➢ Utilize the technique of reframing to see things from a different perspective.

➢ Ask better questions to see things more clearly and in a different light. Ask, "What's great about this?" even in the worst situations.

CHAPTER TEN PREVIEW

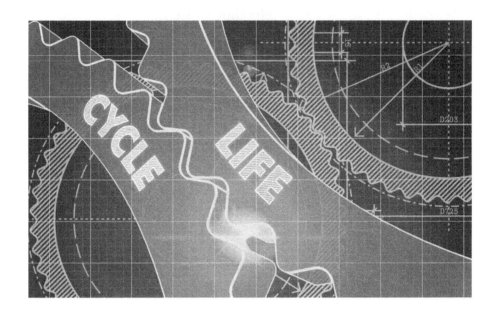

Bring all the pieces together,
and finalize your epic life blueprint!

CHAPTER TEN

Rule Ten: Make it happen, no matter what.

"Winners never quit and quitters never win."
Vince Lombardi

Growing up on a farm, I was asked to handle many chores, and undertake many projects, from putting up barbed wire fences to laying concrete. Whenever we began something new, my Dad would get me started, but he always seemed to leave out a few key details. He left me to figure out how to accomplish tasks on my own.

If I came back to him and said, "Dad, I don't know how to do this," he might give me a pointer or two, but most often he'd say, "Figure it out."

He believed I could do it, and his belief gave me the certainty I was capable, even though I didn't know the specifics. I acted as if I could figure it out, and I did because he believed in me. Each success inspired me to get creative and find ways of doing new things, pushing past my fear of the unknown to get the job done.

When you're committed and creative, either by circumstances or choice, you'll find a way! This is the pathway to confidence. Knowing you can make it happen, no matter what, is the key to having confidence.

When push comes to shove, we get creative; we dig deep and make things happen. Yet, some of us struggle with the urge to throw in the towel much too early in the game when faced with new challenges or a seemingly up-hill battle. If you want success, you're going to have to dig deep and stretch your "make it happen, no matter what" muscle.

When I called my dad from Asia, when my traveler's checks were stolen, he said, "Figure it out." I had no choice but to become creative.

This became a major, foundation experience in my life. I was forced to find my way and muster-up the courage to figure it out on my own.

As I walked back to my hostel with a few dollars in my pocket, I realized my RAS was busy looking for solutions when it drew my attention to a piece of paper on a corkboard. *Looking for English teacher to teach English to Japanese businessmen.* I didn't have teaching experience, but I figured I probably spoke English better than the students, so it was worth a shot. I didn't have anything to lose. I applied and found out all I had to do was have small conversations with the businessmen. It was much easier than one might think, and they paid me $5.00 per hour. I was safe again!

Has that ever happened to you? You assumed something would be difficult, but when you did it, you were surprised at how easy it was.

My confidence went up after this small success. Later that week, I was out with the boys, and they bragged about how much money they were making modeling. We were all North American boys—blond, six-feet tall, fit, with blue eyes. So, I went for it and got another job modeling underwear and running shoes (not at the same time). Now, I was making a living! And I never would have done those things if my father had saved me by sending me the money to come home.

When you're thrust into situations in your life where failure is not an option, and giving up simply won't do, a part of you emerges you never knew existed.

The next time you're afraid and facing a situation you've never faced before, trust yourself to believe you can make it happen, no matter what. Unfortunately, average or struggling people tend to look for the wrong emotional states. Rather than uploading and practicing courage, creativity, nimbleness, flexibility, and openness, they search for the "C" word that kills their chance for happiness and success, or they get angry and blame others, floundering about without doing anything.

Comfort is the thing many people reach for in times of stress. Those who seek comfort never actually experience it. They only achieve a boring, seemingly safer life. But they're quietly dying inside with every chance to grow they let pass them by, and their world and opportunities shrink.

In my case, being stranded in Asia turned out to be one of the best experiences of my life. I learned I could handle anything life threw at me, that I could teach, model, and live in another country. The experience changed my life.

Since then, I've used the phrase "make it happen, no matter what" hundreds of times and fostered a deep belief in myself that I will find a way.

How would your life be different if you had the ability to always find a way, no matter what? Well, guess what? You do. It's in there. You only need to learn to access it.

Let me repeat this because it's incredibly powerful—when faced with the unknown, you'll find a way. If your "why" is clear enough, the "how" will appear. As the expression goes, when the student is ready, the teacher will appear. When the student is willing to practice courage, creativity, nimbleness, flexibility, and openness, anything is possible.

When you develop the mindset to "make it happen, no matter what", you have no plan B. You cannot retreat. You don't allow yourself to go back because it's too compelling to go forward. This is when the champion emerges.

Champions know that put under pressure, with no way out, a part of them shows up because they're willing to go there. They're willing to die for the result they want. In today's world, a choice like this doesn't mean actual death, but once you develop this skill, you become willing to be embarrassed, humiliated, called a crazy person, or a failure, look silly, lose money, or work for education, and start over. You're all in. You'll have the edge over others (and, maybe, over the former you) who have the "I will do it if blank doesn't happen" attitude.

Are you willing to take chances? Are you willing to put yourself on the line, with no backup, and no safety net? If the thought still scares you, reach out and surround yourself with mentors and others who have already done what you're attempting to do, people who are willing to help you.

I've had many coaches in my life, business coaches, health coaches, personal trainers, and spiritual coaches. All of them held my feet to the fire. In Tony Robbins' case, he literally held my feet to the fire, as we did the "fire walk" together many, many times.

Your friends and family are also valuable support systems. As you work through some of the information in this book, you may struggle in certain areas. Maybe you have beliefs you just cannot seem to shake or worries that dog you. In this case, you may wish to seek the advice of a counselor, therapist, or doctor. These resources are there to help you. While you should go into everything you do with a "make it happen, no matter what" attitude, there is no reason you should go it alone.

Take a minute to ask yourself what you're willing to do that will cause you to stretch and grow into the kind of person who'll make things happen, no matter what. If you're still having trouble accomplishing everything you need to do to reach your goals, perhaps you have not fully committed.

Action Steps

- **Commit fully to any decision by taking these four steps:**

Make a decision. Until you make a clear-cut decision, you're not committed. Whatever it is you desire—to lose weight, write a book, start a business, or take your family to Disney World—be crystal clear about it. Know the exact reasons behind your goal. Picture them as if they already are the way you want them to be. Write them down.

Commit to your decision. Get behind it. Humans tend to worry we might be making a bad decision or the wrong choice. A clear decision creates a starting point and gets the wheels turning. A clear decision handles objections up-front, before they occur, with a well-thought-out plan. Successful people know they can always make course corrections and adjustments as they go along.

Pay attention to your thoughts and words. See if you catch yourself saying things like, "I'll take my kids to Disney World one day," or, "I would love to write a book when I have more time." Remember, a decision without a commitment is a dream, a hope, a want, or a wish. There is nothing wrong with dreams. Dreams help us visualize the future and speak the language of our mind in pictures. At the same time, wishing doesn't move you forward, nor does it bring you results. Be committed to your goals, especially in the statements you make to yourself and others.

Declare it. Tell people you love what you've decided to do. Tell others about your goals (the ones who want you to succeed, not the ones who don't get thinking big, or you'll only be forced to manage their fears). This final step is critical because when you let people know what you're going to do, you create a powerful level of accountability by default. You put your reputation on the line. You've also called upon the intangible power of the universe to provide assistance and guidance from these people and others you have yet to meet. Amazing things happen when you make your intentions clear. Declaring your goals and positive affirmations about them to yourself aloud is one of the most powerful things you should be doing daily.

When I was younger, I wanted to be involved in the movie industry. When I learned a movie was being filmed in my hometown of Montreal, I had my chance. I was going to make it happen, no matter what! I went down to the set one morning to apply for a job. They kicked me out, telling me it was a private set. I went back the next day, and a big, burly guy named Tim kicked me off the set again, reminding me it was a private production.

I was a little discouraged, but I kept focusing on my goal and what I wanted to achieve. I went back the next day and ran into Tim once again who said, "Come on, Rock, get out of here. I told you there are no jobs."

"Okay, see you tomorrow," I said, as I was leaving.

This went on for several days, and by the seventh day, my head was filled with thoughts like, "Am I wasting my time? Is this ever going to work? They don't want me. I don't have the skills for the movie business. I'm not good enough."

Despite those voices in my head, I went down again. My reasons for what I wanted were clear. My commitment was total.

That day, as I pulled into the parking lot, Tim told me, "John didn't show up today! Get on in here. You're hired!"

I was ecstatic. This was a genuine, Triple E experience for me, and I've never forgotten the lesson it taught me.

I started out as a gopher, doing odd jobs. As the movie went on, they needed people to fill in the background, to stand around and look like they were at a party. Later, they needed someone to jump off a boat. I ended up in the movie, leaping from a boat as it was smashed in half.

I had unconsciously built a RRAFT and used it to achieve things I hadn't even dreamed about! This was pure evidence that if I was persistent, showed up, and wanted something badly enough, I could attain it.

80% of success is just showing up. It's a sad fact that many people get their first "no" and quit. Knowing this allows me to light a fire under my determination to go above and beyond. The desire to never quit is a skill or characteristic that will get you almost anything you want in your life because so few possess it.

I cannot emphasize this enough! You'll be surrounded by people with half your intelligence, half your education, good looks, and connections, but if they are willing to keep at it, and keep knocking at the door to their dreams, they will achieve more than you. On the other hand, if you choose to adopt the rule of "making it happen, no matter what", you'll be that person people refer to when inspiring others.

I'm not the smartest or best connected person, nor do I've the most education; however, I have a lot of "will not quit", a lot of "go the extra mile", and a lot of "ask, ask, ask, ask". All of this can be learned. Build that fire of desire by focusing on mastering your HISTEP, and watch as you outlast and outperform everyone around you.

My story doesn't end there. I used the skills I had (staying late, doing things no one else wanted to do) to work my way up to assistant director in a B-movie. That one decision, to be persistent and go for what I wanted, led to multiple opportunities. I ended up meeting one of the actresses on the set, dating her, making friends with many people I would never have met, and having some incredible experiences, all because I refused to give up on things I really wanted.

Persistence, determination, and hard work are a mindset. Embrace the mindset of persistence, and you cannot fail.

Ask many successful people, and they'll share stories like mine. They've all worked at becoming the kind of people who refuse to take no for an answer. They commit fully to making it happen, no matter what.

To achieve ongoing success, you first must achieve success in your inner world and develop the character that creates and supports success in your outer world. You have to believe you can figure it out. You must let go of the voices that remind you of times you may have tried and failed in the past.

Tony Robbins said, "The past doesn't equal the future unless you live there." He says, "The strongest force in human nature is our desire to remain consistent with how we see ourselves, as we have been in the past." In other words, what you did yesterday, you'll likely repeat tomorrow because it's what's normal for you. Your income level will remain the same. Your level of passion, love, joy, and laughter will also remain the same unless you take steps to improve them.

One thing is certain; repetition got you where you are today. We've all heard that practice makes perfect. But, that could not be farther from the truth. Practice makes permanent! Our nervous system is designed to create an effortless habit out of behavior performed repeatedly.

This unconscious competence is the ease you seek! The more you practice behaviors designed to help you reach your goals, the easier it will be to figure things out in any situation.

If you allow yourself to "give in", to "give up", and to make your "story" one about why you cannot do something, you'll only repeat your past. Remember, how you do anything is how you do everything.

If you continue perfecting your tennis game, going after the job you desire, or building the relationship you're in, then you make going for it (no matter what, always) the way you are. Period.

One of the best ways to figure things out is with the help of a coach or mentor. Some of my mentors are Anthony Robbins, Butch Harmon, Deepak Chopra, and T. Harv Eker. Modeling a mentor is the shortest path to mastery. Luckily, they've written books you can learn from, and most of them still give seminars you can attend if you don't have the means yet to learn from them privately.

Remember, a road with no obstacles leads nowhere. By setting goals, obstacles will appear. You can either choose your obstacles or life will send them to you. You can solve them alone, or you can do it with the help of experts, mentors, and role models.

Most situations involving the unknown bring fear along for the ride. At these times, it's essential to summon up the courage to move forward. As John Wayne said, "Courage is being scared to death but saddling up anyway."

Persistence does pay. It does pay to dream. It does pay to never give up.

Make it a habit. Don't give up. Don't give into the cry of comfort, but soldier on to be your best self ever. Live your epic life!

Courage is not the absence of fear. It's the presence of commitment and conviction. In life, if you want to make anything happen, you should enter the ring with a spirit of enthusiasm. You must participate fully with a clear sense of direction and purpose. You're a success, long before you reach your goals, just for having fully committed, no matter what.

The more you work on yourself, learning, growing and developing, the more successful you'll be. The happier and more fulfilled you'll be. Problems and challenges in your life, ones that might have taken you out of the game before, will seem relatively small. Why? Because like crawling was once a challenge until you grew up, so will many of the things that seem like challenges today melt away once you begin.

I've given you a wealth of tools in the form of rules, tricks, principles, laws, shortcuts, habits and rituals. Each one survives on its own merit. Yet, put them together and they create a constitution—a code of conduct for success. These are the building blocks for your epic life.

Your epic life blueprint is a source of power and fuel for your endeavors. Your product will be your epic life.

By now, your companion journal or this book should be full of ideas, commitments, and exciting new plans. Review it often. Build upon it, and watch your success grow.

To be successful, you must have a code of conduct that will predetermine your behavior and allow you to keep going, despite the number of times you're going to be told no or when life offers you a setback.

Cultivate the ability to look at things with flexibility. Challenges are going to get in the way. You're going to be at the fair with your kids, and it will start raining. Are you flexible and nimble enough to change? Can you find a solution? Don't be so dead set on one path that you ignore other possibilities. Be flexible. Go with the flow. When trying to figure things out, brainstorm, and listen to all the inputs at your disposal. Explore your options. Be open to them.

Flexibility is crucial to success. If you have a code of conduct predetermining how to act, you can feel secure in your flexibility. You can, by default, program your behavior to lead to good outcomes.

Through repetition, working consistently on yourself, scheduling your time and focusing your energy on the highest payoff activities in relation to your goals, you're building a solid road to your successful and more fulfilled life, to your epic life!

Make these ten rules a blueprint for your success in business and in life. Live life at your full potential, and commit to making it happen, no matter what!

"Life = Risk. If you've never failed, you've never lived."
Rock Thomas

Three Things to Act on

Before completing the next step, look in a mirror and say: "I understand success comes from the implementation of knowledge, not the acquisition of it; therefore, I choose to step into an epic life by taking action on my new-found knowledge. As I read, I will capture the ideas that resonate with me and apply them to my life until I master them. Period. This is what badasses do, and I'm a badass. The result of these committed actions is an epic life!"

Action Step

- **Based on what you learned in this chapter, record three things in your journal or below that you're committed to acting on. Take as much space as you need to outline not only what you'll act upon, but how (steps you'll take), and the all-important why (your reason and result motivations and expectations). Write:**

I commit to take action on:

_____

_____

_____

_____

_____

_____

_____

_____

I commit to take action on:

_____

_____

_____

_____

_____

_____

_____

_____

I commit to take action on:

_____

_____

_____

_____

_____

_____

_____

_____

_____

Chapter Ten Recap

➤ Knowing you can make it happen, no matter what, is the key to confidence.

➤ If your "why" is clear enough, the "how" will appear.

➤ Commit fully to any decision by taking these four steps:

    Make a decision.

    Commit to your decision.

    Pay attention to your thoughts and words.

    Declare it.

➤ 80% of success is just showing up.

➤ The more you work on yourself, learning, growing and developing, the more successful, happy, and fulfilled you'll be.

➤ Having an epic life is up to you! Live life at your full potential.

ABOUT THE AUTHOR

After achieving an elite level of success most only dream about as one of the top fifty realtors in the world, Canadian self-made millionaire, Rock Thomas, re-dedicated his life to helping thousands of people through his seminars, websites, books, and peak-performance coaching programs. Rock is an avid sports enthusiast and family man, currently residing in Montreal, Quebec, Canada.

Visit his website (see all links mentioned in the book, including this one, below).

ROCK'S LINKS

Rock Thomas Website – www.rockthomas.com
Epic Life Blueprint Community –
www.facebook.com/groups/YourEpicLifeBlueprintCommunity
Twitter – twitter.com/rockthomas
Facebook – www.facebook.com/RockThomasOfficial/
Instagram – www.instagram.com/rockthomas/

MASTERMIND GROUPS

M1 – gom1.com
Gobundance – www.gobundance.com

PUBLISHER

Full Sail Publishing – www.fullsailpublishing.com

ALSO BY ROCK THOMAS

The Power of Your Identity

COMING SOON

SAY YES and Figure Out How Later

Special Requests

If you enjoyed this book, please pay it forward by sharing it with a friend and leaving a review. You have the power to help others build epic lives by using a few moments of your time and clicking a rating star. How cool is that?

Your feedback and reviews help me develop new programs and write books that impact the most lives. Each review matters (and I read every one).

My editors are awesome, but they're human. If you find a mistake in the book, please let them know by sending an email to info@full-sailpublishing.com so they can fix it.

If you'd like to talk in person, join the Epic Life Blueprint Community. I look forward to seeing you there and helping you build your epic life blueprint!

With love and gratitude,

Rock

CPSIA information can be obtained
at www.ICGtesting.com
Printed in the USA
LVHW111327210319
611413LV00001B/225/P

9 780991 082353